NO FILTER

NO FILTER

*The Good, the Bad,
and the Beautiful*

PAULINA PORIZKOVA

THE OPEN FIELD · PENGUIN LIFE

VIKING

An imprint of Penguin Random House LLC

penguinrandomhouse.com

The Open Field/A Penguin Life Book

THE OPEN FIELD is a registered trademark of MOS Enterprises, Inc.

The essay "Medicated" was previously published in slightly different form as
"Ending a Midlife Affair with Meds" in *The Huffington Post* in 2011 and the essay "Occupied"
was published in slightly different form as "I Was a Child When Russia Invaded
My Country—and My Mind" in the *Los Angeles Times* in 2022.

LIBRARY OF CONGRESS CATALOGING-IN-PUBLICATION DATA

Names: Porizkova, Paulina, author.

Title: No filter : the good, the bad, and the beautiful / Paulina Porizkova.

Description: [New York] : The Open Field/Penguin Life, [2022] |

Identifiers: LCCN 2022031683 (print) | LCCN 2022031684 (ebook) |

ISBN 9780593493526 (hardcover) | ISBN 9780593493533 (ebook)

Subjects: LCSH: Porizkova, Paulina. | Models (Persons)—United

States—Biography. | Models (Persons)—Sweden—Biography. |

Widowhood—United States. | Women—United States—Social conditions.

Classification: LCC HD8039.M772 .U5369 2022 (print) |

LCC HD8039.M772 (ebook) | DDC 746.9/2092 [B]—dc23/eng/20220801

LC record available at https://lccn.loc.gov/2022031683

LC ebook record available at https://lccn.loc.gov/2022031684

Printed in the United States of America

1st Printing

DESIGNED BY LUCIA BERNARD

Some names and identifying characteristics have been changed
to protect the privacy of the individuals involved.

Dear Reader,

Years ago, these words attributed to Rumi found a place in my heart:

> *Out beyond ideas of*
> *wrongdoing and rightdoing,*
> *there is a field. I'll meet you there.*

Ever since, I've cultivated an image of what I call the "Open Field"—a place out beyond fear and shame, beyond judgment, loneliness, and expectation. A place that hosts the reunion of all creation. It's the hope of my soul to find my way there—and whenever I hear an insight or a practice that helps me on the path, I love nothing more than to share it with others.

That's why I've created The Open Field. My hope is to publish books that honor the most unifying truth in human life: We are all seeking the same things. We're all seeking dignity. We're all seeking joy. We're all seeking love and acceptance, seeking to be seen, to be safe. And there is no competition for these things we seek—because they are not material goods; they are spiritual gifts!

We can all give each other these gifts if we share what we know—what has lifted us up and moved us forward. That is our duty to one another—to help each other toward acceptance, toward peace, toward happiness—and my promise to you is that the books published under this imprint will be maps to the Open Field, written by guides who know the path and want to share it.

Each title will offer insights, inspiration, and guidance for moving beyond the fears, the judgments, and the masks we all wear. And when we take off the masks, guess what? We will see that we are the opposite of what we thought—we are each other.

We are all on our way to the Open Field. We are all helping one another along the path. I'll meet you there.

Love,
Maria Shriver

For Jonathan and Oliver.

Or

Oliver and Jonathan.

The birth order is indisputable, as is my love for you both.

CONTENTS

Preface   *xi*

The Crying Lady on Instagram   *1*

We Were Always Called Girls   *11*

Beauty and the Beast   *19*

Childhood   *29*

The Nature of Beauty   *41*

Falling in Love   *49*

Knowing the Future   *61*

Height   *73*

Magical Money   *85*

The Responsibility of Beauty   *97*

Fame   *105*

Grief and Betrayal   115

Heartbreak   129

Real Money   139

Shock   153

Courage   161

Nude, Not Naked   169

Medicated   181

Occupied   189

Every Woman Is Beautiful   199

Fate and Choice   209

Acknowledgments   219

PREFACE

Years ago, I sat across the table from a journalist, a young woman, as she pulled out her phone to record our conversation. We sipped our lattes and chatted informally before she planned to plunge into her questions. I asked her about herself, something I know interviewers often don't get to talk about. She was all of twenty-two and had just started her job at the magazine. As we talked, she loosened up and said, laughingly: "Yeah, my publisher said, 'Let's get Paulina Porizkova for this, she has no filter and will say anything!'"

No filter. Say anything. So this is how others thought of me.

Certainly, I am unfiltered when it comes to myself. My thoughts. My feelings. I have always been this way. But "say anything"? That gives me no credit whatsoever for keeping the secrets of others. Yet the truth is that I'm weighed down by all the secrets I've kept for other people. Those are mine to keep forever. And so I lighten that load by being unfiltered about myself.

This collection of essays contains things I want to share, things I have thought about, things that hold me back, and things that propel me forward. It is all of me. But it is not a revelation of anyone else. I bring up others only insofar as how they have affected my life.

I spent thirty-five years with my late husband, the most important person in my life, and as such, I have to include him. But he is not here to agree or repudiate my take on things, so this is only my perspective.

And I feel the need to clarify a few points before you leap into these essays with me.

My widowhood and the subsequent events of my life have gotten much attention, and for reasons that have to remain hidden, I must be careful where I tread.

I loved my husband for most of my life, and I always will. But we were separated at the time of his death, although we still lived together and I continued to see him as family. After we had separated, I had fallen in love with someone else and was in a relationship with this man when my husband died. I've never spoken about this publicly, though I've never hidden it either. My friends and family were all aware. My husband knew him, my children knew him, he was an accepted part of our lives. He is unnamed in this book, partly so as not to encroach on his privacy and partly because he no longer needs a name in the story of my life.

When my husband passed away, he left a will in which he stated that I had abandoned him and was therefore not entitled to any part of his estate. The will was drawn up hastily, a few weeks before his death. By using the word "abandonment," my husband wasn't just making a hyperbolic statement—he was making a legal claim. Abandonment of a spouse, legally speaking, is when a person's partner disappears and cannot be contacted for the duration of at least a year. I understand that my husband may have felt abandoned emotionally (although he never let me in on that). But it wasn't the truth. Yes, we were separated. We were in the beginnings of a divorce. Yet we still lived together, we still had family dinners, we still went to dinner parties together as best friends—or so I thought. We laughed about women putting the moves on him, and we talked openly about my boyfriend. We discussed getting apartments close to each other after we sold our home, so our sons could easily go from place to place, and so we could help each other when needed. I thought we had found the perfect way to navigate the end of our marriage, so the will came as an absolute shock. I didn't for a moment imagine I should inherit the full estate. But I thought I would get what one gets in a divorce—half of everything we had acquired together in our thirty-year marriage. But the hastily written addendum to the will made it so I was to inherit much less—and it was based on a lie. This is why I had to pursue a lawsuit, which got settled out of court two years after my husband's death.

No one expected my husband to die. Not his doctors, not his business associates, not his friends, not his family, not me, and not himself. I believe had he known the repercussions that this hasty arrangement wrought on his family, his children specifically, he would have never done it. The will left me in a very strange position of having assets—two large mortgaged houses and our pension plans—but without any income. It pit me against my own business manager and my sons.

Publicly, I was seen as the grieving, wronged widow by many, and a money-grubbing whore by a few. We are all very quick to glorify or vilify, when life is so much more complex than black and white.

My husband will never be able to write his part of this story, so there will never be a perfectly balanced retelling of what actually happened.

I thought I knew him to his bones. I didn't. There were other surprises for me after his death that will stay in my pocket forever, secrets that weigh me down but are not mine to divulge. As are the secrets of many others.

I can tell you only of mine. No filter.

NO FILTER

THE CRYING LADY
ON INSTAGRAM

I was at the opening of a new private club in lower Manhattan, feeling like I'd crashed a party I wasn't invited to. The rooms of polished wood and low lighting were filled with a twentysomething financial crowd, sipping cocktails and throwing back their heads to laugh in a way that seem designed to display the fun they were having. All of them were a good twenty to thirty years younger than me.

As I was heading back from the ladies' room to my table, a young woman at the bar stopped me. She was no more than thirty years old, with long brown shiny hair and a tiny skirt that had hitched up to her upper thighs on the barstool where she was precariously balanced. She was perfectly made-up and slightly inebriated.

"Are you? Are you . . ." She was fumbling around for a name.

Surprised that anyone her age would recognize me, but eager to get back to my table, I smiled and nodded. "Yes, I am." Who she actually thought I was didn't much matter. But as I attempted to maneuver around her, she grabbed my arm.

"Oh my God," she yelled. "You're the lady who cries on Instagram!"

I FIRST BECAME FAMOUS at the age of four, as a political pawn between the West and the East. A year earlier, when I was three years old, my parents left our native Czechoslovakia to escape the invading Soviets. It was 1968. They fled across the border on a motorcycle and eventually ended up in Sweden, hoping for a better life. They had left me with my grandmother, intending to come back for me once they were settled in their new home. But when they tried to return for me, they discovered that the borders were firmly closed. There was no getting their child back. Out of desperation, they did the only thing they could think of: they turned to public opinion. They staged a hunger strike in front of the Czech embassy in Stockholm. They had no connections to money, fame, or power, but they were young, photogenic, and very sad. The Swedish media loved the story, and my parents' campaign to get their daughter back became a sort of reality show, dispensed across newspapers, magazines, and TV appearances.

And so, about once a month for the following five years,

someone from the Swedish press would come to my grandma's house in Prostějov armed with a camera on a Sunday afternoon. As a child, I just assumed all children were having their photographs taken by men who couldn't speak Czech and wore khaki vests with lots of pockets. It wasn't until my best friend looked at me uncomprehendingly when I said I couldn't play that Sunday because the photographers were going to be in town—you know, the ones who always come on Sundays—that I began to realize that my childhood was not typical. It's about the same time I learned that other people's parents didn't all live in Sweden.

Eventually, at the age of nine, when I arrived in Sweden, the newspapers ran stories with my face on the cover: "Poor little Paulina is finally happily reunited with her parents!" Yet it was during this first experience of being so widely "seen" and recognized that I discovered what it meant to not have a voice. My parents had split up the moment we were all reunited, I was longing for the grandmother who had raised me, who had remained back in Czechoslovakia, and I was deeply unhappy at my new school, where the kids called me a dirty Communist. What I felt and what I wanted were irrelevant to the larger story, the one of the "poor" refugee who should have been grateful to have been brought to that country by people's goodwill. No one asked me what I thought.

Those early experiences of being photographed and featured in the news soured me on the idea of being in the public eye.

And yet, at fifteen I moved to Paris to become a model. At the time, it didn't feel like a choice that would shape my whole life. It was just an opportunity to briefly get away from school, where I was the least popular kid. But things have a way of snowballing. I stayed in Paris, dropped out of school, and began a career. At the height of my modeling fame, I'd often have two or more simultaneous covers on newsstands in one month. Around the same time, I fell in love with and ultimately married a musician who was also famous in his own right. But just as when I was a child, I discovered that when I was the most seen, I felt the least heard.

I was used to sell products. Photos and videos of me were indiscriminately altered to best showcase whatever I was selling. In the public eye, I was a manufactured image, not a real person. To be clear, being called one of the most beautiful women in the world was in no way unpleasant. But I felt like an object in a still life. The real me didn't have a voice.

When social media emerged, I, like many others of my generation, was intrigued but baffled by it. I joined Facebook, argued with relatives and friends over politics, and found Twitter. And then, upon the urgings of a dear friend, I joined Instagram.

At first, Instagram was a bit of a shock. Every post had to be visual; there had to be an image of some sort. As I had been a model since I was fifteen, posing for photos was my job. But

I never actually created them, and I never got to choose which one of them was published.

Instagram was a world of self-created content. That gave me a bit of a pause. There was some inherent narcissism in it, and with the pressure that I put on myself to be authentic, it felt intrusive in my life. But I quickly began to realize that Instagram offered me a chance that I'd never had when I worked as a model. It was a chance to give a voice to my face. My voice.

In some ways, my life had never really been my own. First I was known as the little refugee who was happy at last to be reunited with her parents, when in fact I was devastated by the loss of leaving behind everyone and everything I had loved and grown up with. Then I was seen as a celebrated model who had it all, when the truth was that I was a lonely teenager with daily panic attacks. After that, I was the lucky wife in a rare happy celebrity marriage that had beaten the odds, when the truth was that by the time I was fifty, my husband had not touched me for many years.

FOR THE FIRST TIME, I was able to speak directly to whomever wanted to listen on Instagram. I posted photos from modeling jobs, vacations, and everyday life. Along with each photo, I wrote my truth.

Throughout my career, I had always spoken my truth when

asked. I think that because I'd felt so unheard as a child, I always spoke from the heart whenever I was interviewed, even if my attempts to be honest often landed sideways. In one unfortunate incident when I had just turned eighteen, during my first interview for *Us* magazine, a journalist had asked me what I thought of modeling. I had replied with "It sucks." Some people found this cool, some people found it endearing, but many people agreed I was a brat who bit the hand that fed her.

With Instagram, I had another go, this time without the interference of a go-between who'd ask questions and then translate them to best suit the story they wanted to write. Even so, despite my attempts to be completely honest, I still think that many, maybe even most of the people who followed me on Instagram just saw me as a model, and not as a fully formed woman with fears, doubts, joys, and losses.

There was nothing like a real tragedy to humanize me.

MY HUSBAND OF THIRTY YEARS suddenly died. A day later, I found out he had cut me out of his will, claiming I had abandoned him. I was consumed with grief and anger. I could think of nothing else. Every ounce of energy I had went into just functioning in front of my two kids. There was no energy left to make posts about gratitude on Instagram. This is when I began to share my grief. And sometimes my anger. I posted makeup-free selfies. I wrote about the pain. On a few occasions, I posted photos of myself crying.

Those photos shocked people. They commented that I was being performative, that I was objectifying my pain, that I was playing the victim to get others to empathize with me. They said that the kind of self-absorption I had to have to take a photo of myself crying and then post it made me either a narcissist or pathetic.

I will tell you why I posted those crying selfies: I did want empathy. I did want compassion. I was desperate to connect with someone. Anyone. I was crushed by loneliness and isolation. Because pain is a deserted island. My tearful selfies were the messages in the bottle I tossed in the water in an attempt to be heard.

If a desperate need for connection made me a pathetic narcissist in some people's eyes, so be it. But I needed to survive. And it turns out those selfies did connect me to exactly those I was looking for.

Many of my Instagram followers were supportive and sympathetic, and I got a new influx of people who were also grieving and heartbroken, a large audience since everyone was going through a pandemic and the world was a painful place. But many also told me I was embarrassing. They told me to get some meds and shut up. My friends were unnerved and called to check that I wasn't suicidal. Sharing pain made me simultaneously relatable and contemptible.

I came to understand that real stories of pain and failure bring us much closer to one another than any successes. Suddenly I was no longer an image, an object, but a real woman with real pain. Paradoxically, talking about grief, even as it isolates you from many, it connects you with other people who have known grief. But in order to share, we must speak. And we must be heard. I believe this is what it means to be human, to be seen and heard for what and who you are.

We all deserve to be who we are. Being heard is being known, and only by being known can we be loved.

IN THE DIM LIGHT of that private club, with a young woman holding on to my elbow, I marveled at how widely a simple truth could resonate.

"I had no idea who you were, but some of my friends started to follow you." Seeing that she had my attention, she let go of my arm and leaned closer to me. "I saw your crying post— and it changed my life."

The rush to my table and friends was momentarily forgotten.

"My friends tell me to bottle it up, not to make a fool of myself, but sometimes, you know, you don't feel so great. So why do I have to keep pretending everything is fine?"

I nodded.

"I want to thank you," she said, "for sharing your pain. For being real. 'Cause you know, if you can do that, be real and all, then why can't I?"

Just then, her boyfriend walked up and sat on the stool beside her.

She touched his thigh. "Jakey, this is the crying lady on Instagram," she said. Jakey gave me a noncommittal smile. I could tell he didn't give a damn.

But I did. This woman had just given me the best compliment of my life. After all the years of being seen, I was finally heard.

WE WERE ALWAYS
CALLED GIRLS

She was so close I could smell her coffee-and-cigarette breath. It was reassuring. Proof she was human. In this new, unfamiliar, ambiguous world, everyone seemed towering and godlike to me.

The only sources of light in the cavernous studio were the round naked lightbulbs around the mirror. The trestle table under the mirror was laid out with makeup on one side and hair tongs, a blow-dryer, and hair products on the other.

The woman opened half a dozen small glass bottles filled with beige liquids, poured them out on the back of her hand, and blended them with a brush, gauging the color by smudging little bits of the mixture on my chin. When she was satisfied, she stepped close to me, leaned over, and, with the brush, began to apply the color on my face.

It was only my fourth booking, and I was still filled with fear that this would be the day I would be found out; the day I was told that I didn't belong here, that someone made a mistake, that I was no model. I smiled frenetically to assure the makeup artist that I was a nice and accommodating girl. She didn't seem to notice.

I closed my eyes to the flutter of the wet brush against my skin. I heard a door open and peeked from beneath my eyelids. The blackness behind me was momentarily flooded with blue light. A shadow stepped in; then the door closed and the back of the room disappeared into darkness again.

"Bonjour!" the photographer shouted across the room. I had met him only briefly in a go-and-see, but I recognized him immediately and my stomach knotted even harder. By then, I understood that the makeup and hair people and the photography assistants were merely the lesser gods, while the photographer was Zeus, wielding absolute power over his domain. If he didn't like you, you went home. That happened on my second job, shortly after I had been dressed in my first outfit. That photographer, after hurling a bunch of instructions at me in French—which I failed to obey since I didn't understand them—snorted, put his camera down, and, with a wave of his all-powerful hand, dismissed me from the set. I went back to my little room in an apartment that was owned by the director of my agency and cried the rest of the day while I waited to be handed an airplane ticket back to Sweden. Instead I got another job, where the photographer seemed to like me just fine.

Every day, it was a different photographer, different crew, different room. Every day, I had to make new friends and figure out what was wanted from me. Every day, I had to decipher a new language. Every day, I was the new kid in school.

I watched in the mirror as the photographer sidled up behind me and placed something warm and yielding on my shoulder. I kept smiling. The thing on my shoulder looked like a large brown flower in the reflection. I got a whiff of something food-like, soup-like. A soft, heavy pretzel? Pantyhose stuffed with mashed potatoes?

The room was silent except for the pop of an umbrella flash followed by a high-pitched whine as the photo assistant tested the equipment nearby. The makeup artist moved aside a little and laughed. Her laughter assured me this was funny. I joined in, giggling, although I had no idea what I was laughing at.

I kept staring at myself and this odd thing in the mirror. My shoulder was at the same height as the photographer's crotch. Finally, I turned my head to look at it directly and realized it was attached to his body. Attached to the part of his body where a penis would be. It rested there, casually, nestled between my collarbone and the side of my neck. I looked back at us in the mirror.

He grinned at me as if this was a fun little joke. The makeup artist shook her head lightly and raised her eyebrows, as if to say, "Here he goes again!"

I had seen photos and illustrations of penises in health and biology classes at school, but I had never seen a real penis before, and certainly not one held up right next to my face. Could it be?

I wanted to jump up and get away from it. But with another woman laughing, I thought my impulse must be wrong. Her laughter made the whole thing seem . . . lighthearted. Inconsequential. Like I'd ruin the fun if I didn't laugh along. I kept smiling. I needed them to like me.

It wasn't until he retracted that thing on my shoulder, stuffed it back in his pants, and zipped up that I knew for certain that, yes, it really, actually had been his penis.

WHEN YOU ARE A CHILD, you take your cues about your environment from the adults around you. Your mom lets you know this new supermarket is a safe space by the way she calmly navigates it with her cart. Your teacher is at home in her classroom and soon you will be too. A child will find their eventual normal in whatever setting they encounter.

This first encounter with a penis was to be my new normal. I quickly assumed it was a part of the job, and I wasn't wrong.

I long ago lost count of how many times I was greeted by a

photographer in a gaping bathrobe. If it wasn't the photographer, it was a client, or the nephew of a client, or one of the client's friends. It happened so often it became just another day on a shoot. In fact, if a photographer well-known for being creepy didn't try something, I'd feel uneasy, insecure. It meant that I wasn't as attractive as the other girls who were getting harassed. Harassment, perversely, became a confirmation of desirability.

Being a model was about inspiring desire in the photographer—who was, nearly all of the time, male. If the photographer was a straight man, it was about inspiring sexual desire. If he was gay, it was about embodying an abstract idea of beauty. You had to become a work of art, a sculpture, a painting. In either case, you had to become a man's idealized version of a woman: beautiful, sexual, perfect.

The sexual tension at a shoot wasn't a side effect. It was something you wanted, because it would make for better photos. I knew how to create sexual tension well before I'd actually had sex. Even so, there was a photographer who once shouted at teenaged, virgin me, "Look at me like you want me to cum!"

I asked, "Come where?"

He never booked me again.

Now, as a fifty-seven-year-old woman, it's not lost on me that the sexualized ideal woman you saw on the covers of magazines forty years ago did not know a penis when it was literally pulled out right in front of her face. Because the ideal woman was not a woman at all. She was a girl.

IN MODELING, careers start young and often end young. When you are taught the rules as a child, you don't question them. I was told models had to be young, because their smooth skin reflected light in a way that older faces did not. But I suspect there is another, darker reason for having seventeen-year-olds hawking antiwrinkle creams.

All models were and still are called girls. Regardless of age. Why are there no women in modeling?

Because a girl doesn't know to say no. A girl does not know her own power. A girl does not know her value. Because she wants people to like her, she puts up with things she never should have.

And yet, what is held up as the ideal of physical womanhood today—the perky full breasts, tiny waist, perfectly rounded behind, large eyes, tiny nose, full lips, thick hair, and smooth skin of a child—these are the attributes of a teenager.

We have created a giant industry of antiaging products and a booming plastic surgery business that subsist on our insecurities. I myself was a part of this, selling the dream of youth to a world hungry for it. I sold antiaging creams to women closer to my mother's age when my skin was effortlessly taut. I sold calendars with my mostly unclothed body to men who were old enough to be my father, when I was just growing into that exposed body. I didn't know any better. What teenager does? I was a part of a well-oiled machine set in motion long ago. As a child, I didn't question the rules.

Now, as a woman in her fifties with a life well lived and many lessons learned, I've come to find out I'm still supposed to look like the girl who doesn't know what a penis is.

The danger isn't just in setting up that impossible beauty standard. It's in what that standard represents and demands of women. Which is that we not only look like girls, but act like them too. If the ideal woman is seventeen, then the ideal woman is naive, malleable, inexperienced, and undiscerning. The ideal woman is not a woman. She's a girl.

BEAUTY AND
THE BEAST

As I lay in bed next to him, our legs intertwined, our arms thrown across each other on the white sheets, we probably looked like spaghetti on a plate. All long limbs, tangled up: whole wheat tossed with semolina. I always marveled at the color difference of our skin—even in winter, I was at least three shades darker. I thought we looked beautiful together. And I thought Ric was the most beautiful man in the world.

He was six-four and very thin, but it was a slimness that was natural, not starved. I loved the planes and angles of him, the architecture of him. His long, powerful runner's legs. His flat stomach. His elegant neck. His proud nose. It all came to life with his eyes, an unusual shade of turquoise. I'd lie in bed and study his irises. There was a hint of yellow around the pupil and cornflower blue at the edge of the iris. These color variations in the small space of an eye made them change shades in different light, from pale blue to gray to turquoise and even to green. These beautiful eyes he kept hidden from most people with his ubiquitous sunglasses. And he had the softest lips.

We got up slowly, leisurely, made a pot of coffee, and opened the fridge to discover we needed to make a trip to the supermarket. For most people this is a boring common chore, but for us, it felt a little bit like going into battle. I could easily keep my thick glasses on and my hair in a topknot, dress in sweats, and pass mostly unnoticed. But Ric, with his height, his distinctive mop of dyed black hair, and his permanent uniform of head-to-toe black clothing, was a walking upside-down exclamation mark. He looked exactly as he did in all his music videos, which were playing nonstop on MTV at the time—making him instantly and easily recognizable anywhere we went.

The A&P market was a few blocks away. As soon as we left our front door, our hands found each other, like magnets. We managed to walk down the block before a family of three stopped us.

"Oh my God, the dude from the Cars, right?" the father shouted at Ric, stopping right in front of us so we couldn't move ahead.

"Can I have your autograph? We're such huge fans! My boy, here, Dylan, especially." He pushed his son forward a little. About twelve, his son looked at his shoes as if hoping he could make himself vanish.

I could feel Ric exhale. His mouth tightened, just a little. He gave a small nod and reached out his hand for paper and pen.

The man reached into the pockets of his cargo shorts, as though he regularly kept paper and pens in them, and came up short. "Uh, dude, sorry. Do you have a pen and paper?" He was wearing a T-shirt with Bruce Springsteen's face printed on it, and the T-shirt kept riding up his belly. He was sweating profusely and kept tugging the T-shirt down in his excitement.

"Sorry." Ric shrugged. He grabbed my hand to keep walking, but the man wouldn't let him go so easily.

"No, wait! Stop!" he shouted at us, as his wife went for a mad scramble in her handbag. We waited until she extricated a packet of tissues, apparently the only paper she had. She handed it to Ric.

"I'm sorry," he said, motioning emptily with his hand, "I do not have a pen."

The wife and the husband frowned. Ric tried to hand the tissues back. "No, no, no," the man protested. "Just give me a sec. Dylan is such huge fan!"

Dylan looked mortified while his father started asking

passersby for a pen. His wife stood in place, smiling at Ric. "It's such a pleasure to meet you," she said to him. "We're from Ohio, and imagine, we get to meet a celebrity just walking down the street in Manhattan."

I smiled at her, but she didn't even glance at me. Since she didn't notice me, I got to observe. She was pretty, with freckles and big brown eyes. Her blond hair was pulled into a severe ponytail with bangs frozen in a cresting stiff wave. She had oddly plucked eyebrows, the front parts closest to the bridge of her nose thick and dark, and the rest of the brows trailing off in a thin, wispy tail. Sort of like two sperm. I gave her a makeover in my mind, letting her hair down and brushing it smooth and penciling in those brows. Her husband, balding and red-faced, had married a prize, I thought.

"Mom, can we go now?" Dylan tugged at her sleeve. He looked like his mother, I thought, with blond hair and beautiful brown eyes. Finally, the husband found someone willing to lend him a pen, and Ric did his signature scrawl on the plastic package of the tissues.

"Oh, could you sign the tissues too?"

Ric pulled out tissue after tissue. I let him place the tissues on my back so he could have support to write on the flimsy paper.

Finally satisfied, the family thanked Ric profusely. They had never once acknowledged my existence. As we walked away, we could hear Dylan say, "Dad, who *was* that?"

I ADDED OUR PREFERRED Colombian coffee beans to our shopping cart, along with plain yogurt, blueberries, paper towels, toilet paper, and whole milk, and I wandered over to the produce department to find cantaloupes, Ric's favorite breakfast food. Personally, I thought cantaloupes tasted like soap, but Ric convinced me they were super healthy, so I was getting used to eating them daily as well.

Ric had already signed three more autographs in the supermarket and was now in a corner while someone was taking a photo of him with their girlfriend. I picked up a melon and gently squeezed it, then held the stem to my nose for that telltale "it's ripe" scent.

"Excuse me," someone said next to me. I looked up from the cantaloupe. It was a young man, beautifully dressed in a light blue shirt and white jeans. "Are you, you're . . . Paulina Po . . . what's her name?" I nodded and put down the melon so I could do the required autograph.

"No, you're not," the guy said, setting a hand on his hip.

I was trying to pick a melon, not a fight. "Okay, so, no, I'm not," I said.

"Yes, you are!" he shouted, as if I had suddenly given myself away.

I picked the melon back up. "Okay, I am."

Now he looked doubtful again. "But are you? Really?"

I exhaled with frustration. I turned to him, took off my glasses, and shook my hair out.

He gasped. "You are!"

I expected him to ask for that obligatory autograph, but instead he poked at me playfully. "Girl, you could use a bit of lipstick and mascara," he said, and walked away.

RIC HAD FINISHED the impromptu photo session and made his way over to me, holding a can of tuna, Miracle Whip, and slices of Kraft cheddar for his favorite midnight snack sandwich, all of which he tossed into our cart. We headed for the register. There was a bit of a line, so while we waited, Ric kept signing autographs and nodding to people who shouted, "I love you," or that the Cars "sucked." I picked up a copy of a gossip magazine and absentmindedly flipped the pages. And there, there, was a photo of me and my beloved, at some premiere or another, our arms around each other, smiling and happy. Above the photo, in black blocky text: BEAUTY AND THE BEAST. The words knocked the breath out of me. I quickly snapped the magazine shut.

But Ric had noticed something was going on. "Let me see that."

He took the magazine from me, looking for the page. Waves of shame and anger washed over me. What an awful thing to say about someone. How could they? My boyfriend was beautiful. It was true that his beauty was unusual, almost alien, but that was exactly why I found him so beautiful. He was distinct, original. He was a Modigliani, not a baseball card.

We moved forward and I started to toss our groceries onto the counter. Over my shoulder I saw him find the page, look over it, close the magazine, and stick it back into the magazine rack. The cashier scanned our items without looking up. Ric stepped around me to load a plastic bag. Our eyes met. I didn't know what to say, so I tried for a smile and an eye roll. I felt . . . guilty. Like I had done something wrong. At the same time, my mind was furiously ticking through other model/rock star couples—Keith and Patti, Billy and Christie—and wondering who the hell was setting these arbitrary beauty standards. How were Billy Joel or Keith Richards better-looking than my boyfriend? The couple we had just met also sprung to mind. I wondered if the pretty brown-eyed wife found her sweaty husband beautiful. If anyone should be called "beauty and the beast," it was them, I thought. And then I wondered if anyone ever said that out loud about them, the way people felt free to say the same out loud about me and Ric. I felt a flash of anger at that couple. Why were Ric and I made fun of while they got to live their lives in peace?

You'd think that the experience of being so harshly judged in the public eye would make us less likely to judge others.

But that isn't true at all. Being judged did not teach me to be nonjudgmental. On the contrary, it made me more critical. Being judged made me sharper, meaner. I felt such a heavy burden of judgment that I tried to balance the scales of that judgment by judging others, instead of acknowledging that it was the scale itself that was the problem.

Ric did the same. There was no sharper critic. Men who wore their baseball hats backward and cargo shorts were at the very top of his long list of dislikes. Dismissing others made us feel better about ourselves amid the onslaught of criticism we faced: "How did he possibly get her? What does she see in him? Would she still love him if he wasn't a rock star?"

We comforted each other by convincing ourselves that the two of us were shiningly, perfectly, blindingly better than all those who dared to criticize us. We had a perfect view from the top of our mountain. So what if the top of the mountain was a bit windy? A bit lonely? We needed no one else. And that was a good thing, for no one else could possibly ever climb up to meet us with all the rocks we threw down at them.

In the checkout line, Ric had packed our groceries and picked up the bags.

"I'm sorry," I said softly.

He stepped toward me, transferred both bags to one hand, and slung the other around my shoulders. He gave me a squeeze. "Don't worry, honey," he said. "I don't think you're a beast."

———

SHORTLY BEFORE GETTING PREGNANT with my first son, I was working on a movie in which I had a small part in a cast of many other actors, some very famous, some very famously difficult. One famous actor kept making a real effort to hang with the crew, from the teamsters to the electricians to craft service. Everyone loved him. That set was an ego explosion, but in the midst of a roiling ocean of battling personalities, he was an island of calm. By being kind to the people around him, he made his little slice of the world better.

It was the seed of an idea, of how I could be in the world— a seed that didn't take root and grow until years later, when my husband and I separated. That's when I made a conscious choice to be a different person. Every time I felt that old urge to judge someone, I would step back and ask myself why. Why did I want to belittle someone else? Invariably, it was to make myself feel better by comparison. So, I did the reverse. I wished them well. I applauded them. I had fallen into a habit of judgment, and now I had to create a new habit of generosity.

This is a learned skill, and I have by no means perfected it. It's difficult, and I struggle with it sometimes. I still have my bitchy moments.

But I agree with my husband. I am no beast.

CHILDHOOD

CHILDHOOD

W here is my home? Where is my home?" is the opening line of the Czech national anthem. When I think of home, I think of the house where I grew up on 33 Rejskova Ulice. It sat squarely along with its neighbors of neoclassical stone town houses in shades of soft yellow, beige, and cool gray. Above the windows and doors were intricate stone carvings of vines and scrolls. The glass in the tall windows was old, wavering and melting, perfectly bisected by the type of crossed mullions you would see in a child's drawing. Heavily carved walnut doors stood at the top of two stone steps, whose corners were rounded with age. In the early summer, the soft chamomile smell of the flowering linden trees that shaded the street permeated everything. Our street was right off the main square in the middle of my small town, Prostějov. This was my heart, the place I belonged.

It didn't matter that the beautiful stone was covered by a layer of grime. The grime muted and softened the divisions between the individual houses, made them flow into one another. It didn't matter that we had no hot water, a toilet housed on the veranda, and stoves heated with coal. It didn't matter that seven of us shared a single bedroom. It didn't matter that we took only one bath a week—in a long tin tub my grandpa pulled out of the basement on Sundays. My grandmother, my babi, had to heat pots of water on the old black cast-iron stove in the kitchen, the behemoth that was used for both cooking and heating. We would bathe in turns, starting with the kids, my cousin and I, and go in order of age. Grandpa, being the oldest, got the dirtiest and coldest bathwater.

My home, the sweetness of my childhood, resided in this old town house with the reassuring smell of mold in the damp stone basement, the high-ceilinged first and second floors, and the lofty bright attic where Babi hung the laundry to dry between old sun-warmed wooden beams that scented the air with a sweet cinnamon smell.

The house had been inherited from an uncle of my grandpa. After World War II, the Communist government judged it too spacious for one family and divided it. My family lived on the first floor, while the second floor was divided between two households. A tiny little room on the second floor was home to Pani Rusova, a woman of a mysterious age and mysterious history. She had no plumbing in her room and had to come downstairs to use the toilet on the veranda and fill buckets with water from the cold-water tap in the kitchen. The rest of the second floor was a one-bedroom apartment mirroring our apartment downstairs, occupied by another family.

Later, when my mother, my little brother, and I moved to Sweden, I'd have my own room in a modern apartment building on the outskirts of town. It was a boxy, redbrick, three-story building filled with single moms and alcoholic men. There were no decorations above the windows, or doors, or anywhere. The buildings were square and utilitarian. Inside, a long dark hallway opened to square rooms on either side, bedrooms on one side and living areas on the other. It was very clean, very sparse. My brother and I each had a bunk bed and a desk. The living room had a mustard-colored pleather couch set that glued your thighs to it and made a wet peeling noise when you stood up. A big round paper ball lantern hung from the ceiling, casting a shadowless flat light.

Our building was wedged between a gas station and a dark little supermarket. The apartment building was somehow built on the only hill in town in the midst of the flattest landscape you could imagine, so entering it from the front, you needed to climb a flight of stairs to get to our apartment. In the back, however, our balcony off the kitchen was on level ground. I often used this balcony as a way to get in and out.

Once I moved out on my own, I always preferred high-ceilinged, impractical places to modern comfortable ones.

"WHEN YOU PUT a paper and a pen before a child and ask them to draw a house, all of them, *all of them*, will draw the little square with the triangle roof, the door in the middle, and two windows on the sides. A chimney. Maybe a sun and a flower. But the house is always the same," a psychologist once explained to me at a party. We found ourselves, just the two of us, outside on a patio, having the sort of intense conversation that occasionally happens between strangers at parties.

"Now, this child needs to inhabit this house. It's where the child belongs. There are no other options. So, imagine this child walking to the house to get home and the front door is closed. Locked. The child can't get in. Well, then the child will try the right window. If it's locked too, the child will try the left window. If that is also locked, the child will try any other option. Even the chimney. Once the child has learned that the chimney is the way into the house, this will always be their entrance. It doesn't matter that it takes a lot longer, that it's dangerous and inconvenient. It doesn't even matter if the front door and the windows are later flung open—the child will always choose the chimney."

In that moment, I realized I had been taking the chimney into the house for most of my life. In the house I built, I had not even bothered to install a front door. I put a staircase to the chimney instead.

Our childhood years are called formative for a reason. They shape us to become the people we are. We now know that unconditional love from parents builds a solid sense of self-worth, and the opposite is true as well. Most of us fall somewhere in the middle.

My parents left me when I was a child to find us a better life. They were young and idealistic and had no idea things wouldn't work out the way they wanted. I grew up with my grandparents, my grandmother a substitute for my mother. I may have been growing up under Communism's heavy hand, wearing cast-off clothing and waiting in endless lines with my babi for a single banana at Christmas, but I still consider my childhood the happiest years of my life. The outside deprivation of material things was not at all important to my happiness. My babi loved me unconditionally, and I was safe.

WHEN I WAS in my early forties, I finally began therapy to help address my lifelong anxiety. Being in therapy helped me understand that I had married a man very much like my father, the father who vanished from my life when I was three, when he and my mother left Czechoslovakia for Sweden. We were never truly reunited. The first night we spent together as a family, after years of separation, was in a hotel room in

Vienna. We were all on our way to Sweden. That first night back together, my father told my mother he had fallen in love with someone else. They thought my little brother and I were asleep on our cots, but I heard it all. My mother sobbed, but I thought, "Good, now I can go back to Babi."

Like my husband, my father was tall, talented, and elegant, with dark hair and light eyes. And like my husband, the world had to revolve around him. But it took me a very long time to realize that my husband, Ric, was also very much like my babi, the grandmother who loved me completely and utterly, and then, through no fault of her own, disappeared from my life.

When I was little and made a mess, or came home with a bad grade, or forgot to put my dirty pants in the laundry, she would grab her head and stoop over, the weight of the world crushing her, and declare that today was the day she would throw herself under a train. When I was older, my cousin and I would flippantly remind her that the train station was just down the block, but when I was little, I took this quite literally. I would cling to her leg and beg her not to kill herself.

I was her baby, her last child to raise. Her love was an ocean that encompassed me. I felt like I was the only person she loved. Babi; my grandfather; my youngest aunt; my oldest cousin; my youngest cousin, who was only fourteen days older than me; and I all lived together. But Babi never hid the fact that she loved me differently. She loved me more.

Ric never threatened to off himself à la Anna Karenina, as Babi did. He was never histrionic like her. He was cool, collected, and gentle. For a long time, I thought the two of them were nothing alike, that they were opposites. But I see now that he had the same sort of possessiveness and obsessiveness. I recognized it not as controlling but as loving. This was the chimney into love that I recognized.

WHEN I WAS SEVEN, my mother, pregnant with my little brother, returned to Czechoslovakia with the help of a Swedish newspaper to try to kidnap me and bring me back to Sweden with her. She was caught and imprisoned. She was allowed to visit me once a week, accompanied by two police officers. After one of these visits, my mother refused to go back, and the police allowed her to stay under house arrest in my grandparents' home. This arrangement continued for the next three years. The Swedish newspaper that had bankrolled this plot had an even better story than they could have hoped for. Now it wasn't just poor little Paulina trapped with the Communists. Now it was poor little Paulina, her innocent baby brother, and her badass mother all trapped. Eventually, the Czech government tired of the terrible publicity (our family's plight caused a scandal when the Swedish hockey team threatened to refuse to play the Czechs in the 1972 Ice Hockey World Championships) and ejected us. Our citizenship was revoked, and we were told we were never to return. I was finally going to meet my father. In Sweden.

INITIALLY, when my parents took off to find a better life and left me behind, I wasn't sad or scared. I figured, with a child's easy logic, that they left me behind because they didn't want me. It was okay though: my babi did.

When my mom came back, I was really excited, until I noticed she didn't have much time for me, always having to attend to my crying newborn brother. And she herself seemed to be in a constant bad mood, crying or shouting at me. A child has no idea there are other events shaping their parents' lives besides themselves. There was no way for me to understand my mother's fears; she had been given amnesty, which meant only that her prison sentence was temporarily suspended. There was no way for me to know my grandfather's cough was caused by cancer, which was slowly killing him. At the age of seven, there was no way for me to empathize with the madly shifting hormones of a woman who had just given birth.

But my babi always had time for me.

Three years after my mother arrived, we were released to go to Sweden. As a ten-year-old, I had no idea what that really meant. Babi couldn't stop crying, and I tried to console her, reminding her with complete assurance that I would be back for summer vacation. This just made her cry more, because she, of course, knew that was not likely to happen. I did not.

When we left Czechoslovakia, I was separated from the only person who I knew loved me unconditionally and completely. I didn't know it then, but in leaving Czechoslovakia and leaving Babi, I also left behind my belief that I was lovable.

THE RESULT OF USING the chimney to get home throughout my childhood was that I thought this way was the only way to love, to belong. I diligently took the same way in as a young woman.

"You actually found the perfect person to love you. You found a man who not only was your parents but your grandmother as well," my therapist pointed out.

I'd found the trifecta of crooked chimneys.

I WONDER IF I'll always be building a ladder to a chimney. Can I change? Can I change how I get into the house? Can any of us? Any of us who find ourselves having fallen in love with someone because of the patterns of childhood, who now realize that the pattern is unsustainable, can we change? There are a lot of us out there. Are we committed to making the same mistakes over and over because of a locked front door in earliest childhood?

I have a theory. For heteronormative people, the parent of the same gender is who you, intentionally or not, model yourself after. The parent of the opposite gender is who you'll fall in love with. Sometimes, the qualities will intermingle, and you'll find your partner in fact possesses the qualities of both your parents. This is certainly true for me and in my conversations with my friends. If a man's mother is bossy or moody or cold or capable or charming, he will find a woman with some of those qualities, and it will feel like chemistry to him. He'll be attracted without quite knowing why. If a woman's father is explosive or funny or a tightwad or gentle or a liar, she may likewise recognize these characteristics in her loved one.

Of the two men I've loved, one was like my father, one was very much like my mother. And I must, with a bit of reluctance, confess that both of the men I've fallen deeply in love with had cold, distant, and artistically inclined mothers.

The people you grow up with shape your understanding of love. Your little house built in childhood represents the love we're talking about. You can't tear down the house. You can learn there are other ways into the house, easier ways to access the love you want. You can find the courage to try the door. This is what I have been trying to do for years now, what everyone I know has encouraged me to do.

I understand the concept of the front door. But I don't see it. I still want to take the ladder up to the fucking chimney.

For a long time, I thought this was a problem, this fact that

I couldn't see the front door, the fact that the climb up the chimney was my only way in to love. I've been beating myself up for most of my life because I couldn't find the right way in as a child. Everyone has pointed this out to me: that my way to get in is the wrong and most complicated way possible. But the truth is that my childhood house with Babi was filled with love, and my married home with Ric was filled with love too. It's true I may have built a staircase to the chimney—not the world's most practical solution—but my hard-to-access house was nevertheless filled with love.

Babi's house at 33 Rejskova may have been shabby and smudged with coal soot. The tin tub in the middle of the kitchen, where my babi would pour pots of warm water over my head, was the safest, most loving place I have ever been. Nothing bad could happen there, in that threadbare, beautiful old home.

And chimneys can be beautiful too. Even if they're harder to access. They're still a way in. My way in.

Just because you use the chimney as a front door doesn't mean that you won't be happy and feel joy and love. It just means you need to climb.

Our deep flaws and ridiculous needs brought Ric and me together, yes. But the love in that house also brought twenty-five years of a happy marriage.

Maybe going through the front door is not possible for everyone. Maybe I just need to find someone who also goes through the chimney, a partner who also sees a chimney as a front door. Or a partner who can patiently watch me with a smile as I climb up on the roof, knowing we'll both meet inside. Is it harder to climb the rickety ladder to the high roof and crawl down a narrow and crooked chimney? Yes, of course it is. Do I wish it were easier for me to access the love I want? Yes, but I don't know any other way. It seems the important thing is that the house you eventually enter is full of love. The way in we learned as children may be impractical, but it can get you to where you belong.

THE NATURE
OF BEAUTY

I woke up and realized my life was over.

A deep, red, and achy pimple loomed on my chin. It was one of those insidious ones: huge, raised, very visible, but not poppable. Sweat broke out under my newly shaven and still tender underarms.

I transported myself and my pimple to the photo studio, with my scarf wrapped up to my nose. Keeping the pimple hidden with a scarf worked on the subway, but it wasn't an option here. Two other girls were already sitting by the makeup mirror, freshly washed, depilated, and flawless. As the makeup artist greeted me, I unwound my scarf with a sense of absolute doom.

Her eyes bulged. "Ooh la la," she exclaimed. "What are we going to do?"

I stood, shame washing over me as she summoned the clients and the photographer. Everyone gathered around me. The makeup artist grabbed my face, turning it this way and that to show everyone how the pimple stuck out, telling them how she could cover the redness but couldn't get rid of the lump. I would probably have been better received had I arrived covered in vomit, because that at least one could wash off. Now what?

They all convened in a dark corner, whispering and pointing at me. By consensus, it was then determined the makeup artist would give it a try. Maybe there were angles that, in tandem with makeup, could work. The two other girls looked at me with pity. And a little satisfaction. More photos for them.

After an hour of makeup, which only seemed to magnify the massive lump on my chin, a black-clad stylist with a cigarette clamped in the corner of her mouth dressed me in a white-sequined bustier and led me to the set. Another model was sitting there, finishing up. She sat on a stool, her jeans and dirty Converse sneakers peeking out from under the tulle of a wedding dress. Her tiara, the object of the photo, was perched on her perfectly coiffed hair—what the rest of her looked like was unimportant. My heart sank further. We were doing close-ups of wedding headgear. My pimple would be impossible to disguise. A few more clicks of the other model, and I was shoved into the vacated chair.

I had frequently felt ugly, certainly in school—where I'd

been mercilessly bullied—and often on go-and-sees, where my flaws were discussed before me as though I couldn't hear what they said, but this was another level. Modeling is all about pretending. Pretend you're not cold, pretend you're not about to faint from heat, pretend that you love this lipstick, pretend you are delighted to be here. But how do you pretend to be beautiful? The photographer clicked a few dispirited frames, and I was dismissed from the job.

THIRTY YEARS LATER, when I was in my late forties, I met with my former agent to talk about my modeling career. I hadn't seen her for years, since I hadn't been working as a model. Instead, I had branched off into movies and writing.

"It's not like I want to resurrect my career," I said, sipping my latte, "but—" I never got to finish that thought, because she interjected with laughter.

"Oh lord, that is not even a faint possibility."

I put my cup down. My agent was not the kind of woman to crush a dream with a laugh over a coffee. If anything, she had always been reassuring and enthusiastic. But truthful. She had always been truthful.

Until that moment, I hadn't realized that I had most definitely aged out of my business. I had been so focused on doing things I loved—for very little money—I didn't realize that the modeling gigs, which were my primary money source,

had withered and died. Not because I had neglected that career, but because of my age.

Like the evil pimple, my wrinkles were now a major flaw
that prevented me from being regarded as beautiful enough to
be photographed to sell things. A pimple could be gotten rid
of, and so, in a way, could wrinkles. All they required was a
vial of Botox, which could turn my face as smooth and expres-
sionless as a newly hatched egg.

The two most profitable areas in a dermatology office are
acne and wrinkles. Acne is a bacterial infection of the skin,
treated as a disease, while wrinkles are a permanent witness to
you having lived long enough to acquire them. Yet both are
seen as definite flaws. Both need to be treated.

BUT HOW DO YOU fix nature's progress? How can you com-
pare the flower buds of a tree in spring to the amazing lush
greenery of summer, to the fiery leaves of autumn, to the stark
chiaroscuro of winter? We understand those changes are ir-
revocable, and each one delights in its own way.

A YEAR AGO, I was on a shoot for a magazine. I stood before
the white paper background of a typical photo studio, somewhere in Brooklyn, with my artfully tousled hair and minimal
makeup, and I forgot I was a fifty-six-year-old woman. My

body and face kicked into muscle memory of so many years past. I posed and mugged and pouted and laughed at the camera as I had always done. It wasn't until I saw the photos published that I realized how much I had changed. I looked like a woman. An older woman. The camera had captured my wrinkles in a way that my iPhone never did. A stark black-and-white close-up of me showed me what I really looked like. And I was horrified. I needed Botox. I needed fillers. I needed a damn face-lift.

But for what? To look like I used to. To look unchanged.

I WISH I COULD SAY that I'm happy with looking my age. I wish I could tell you that I am at a point of blissful peace about my wrinkles and have accepted how I look now. But I haven't. It's a daily struggle of self-acceptance. I have to keep reminding myself that it's what happens when you're lucky enough to get older. You know how you don't get wrinkles? You die young.

I AM NO LONGER SPRING. I am late summer ceding into the magnificent colors of fall. What if I embraced this change instead of trying to hold on to the past? What if I claimed this face with all its changes and proclaimed it beautiful even if I am struggling with it?

I posted a photo from the Brooklyn photo shoot to my Instagram account, along with my reflections about my insecurities. I chose the one that caused me the most discomfort, a stark black-and-white close-up of my face, every line, every sag magnified by the camera.

It got 7,077 comments, one of the highest number of comments for anything I've ever posted. Women started sharing their stories about insecurity. About struggling to accept their own faces as they age. Grateful that there was someone else, someone with a megaphone, who felt like them. It was as if I held a little lantern and walked down an unlit path. They could follow me.

THINK OF BEAUTIFUL THINGS. Flowers. Clouds. Trees. Sunsets. Nature makes them fleeting and ever-changing in their beauty. Their transience is a part of the enchantment. A fresh summer morning is as beautiful as a hot sunny afternoon, which gives way to a glorious sunset, followed by a velvety night sprinkled with stars. Each one is beautiful for what it is. We may have favorites, but there is beauty in all of it.

Everything in nature changes. But as people, we have a tendency to hold on to things, to refuse to allow change. Like objects—paintings, cars, watches—we pay for the things we love to remain the same forever. We want them to continue being what we bought. They are our possessions. If a painting cracks, we will fix it. If it can't be fixed, it's broken and worthless.

This is where the objectification of women is most apparent. Our beauty is, like nature, ever-changing—but the world insists upon our beauty remaining static. If we were not seen as objects, we would be allowed to change. Even celebrated. We would be celebrated for aging.

FALLING IN LOVE

One late night in 1984, I found myself mesmerized by a singer in a music video. I had just gotten cable, and my then-boyfriend insisted the TV stay permanently tuned to MTV. I usually didn't even notice what was going on on-screen. But this time, I could not look away.

The singer was languidly sprawled out on a couch, thin and elegant with thick black hair, dazzling aquamarine eyes, and large ears that stuck out in an endearing way. There was a woman in the video, too, a rather conventionally hot blonde. I immediately disliked her. But him, my God, *him*. He seemed so confident, and also awkwardly beautiful in his movements. There was a moment of a close-up of his face, in which, for a fraction of a second, I detected a smile, the hesitant smile of a vulnerable little boy. That's what really got to me.

I turned the volume all the way up and sat on the edge of my uncomfortable couch. The room echoed with the music. My boyfriend wasn't home, so it was just me, my cat Mephisto, and our new puppy, a golden Lab named Midas. Midas needed to go out, but he would have to wait.

The song title and artist appeared in the corner of the screen: "'Something to Grab For': Ric Ocasek."

I gasped a little. His last name was Czech. All Czech last names, the old names that didn't come from Germany, mean something very specific. "Porizkova" means—well, it's a little hard to translate, but the closest I can come up with is "the one who belongs to a large man who eats a lot." His name, Ocasek, means "little tail." How absolutely adorable. And also, familiar. I had a new celebrity crush.

A FEW MONTHS LATER, I found myself sitting on the floor of a living room in the Four Seasons hotel. It was a very brown room, not particularly dazzling. I was shooting a music video the following day, and the band and I were gathered around the coffee table. I'd never heard of the band before but had assumed the members would be younger—closer to my age. The men sitting on the sofas all looked like they were in their thirties. I was nineteen. We had said hello, introduced ourselves, and now we just sat in uncomfortable anticipation. I had been told the band would take me to dinner, and I was hungry. After a bit of small talk I piped up: "Are we waiting for something?"

"We're waiting for Ric. He should be right out."

As if summoned telepathically, the door from the adjoining room opened, and in walked, holy fucking shit, the man from the video. Ric Ocasek.

WATCHING HIM WALK ACROSS the room toward me, I knew this was the man I was going to marry. He made a beeline for where I sat and, without a word, got down on the floor next to me, folding up his long, lanky body and staring right into my eyes. Still silent. I began hyperventilating.

Finally, I said, "Please don't pay any attention if I faint. I'm just really nervous."

Without ever taking his eyes off my face, he gently touched my knee.

"If you faint, I'll catch you."

My anxiety, which had been spooling out like a fishing line attached to a fast-moving shark, started reeling back in. He hadn't laughed at me, or dismissed me, or viewed me as *damaged*. I suddenly felt safe.

He had caught me and held me. And he continued to hold me, keeping me safe, for the next twenty-five years.

———

FALLING IN LOVE is a bit like having a temporary mental illness. (In fact, recent studies of brain scans show that being in love causes changes in the brain that are strikingly similar to serious health problems like drug addiction and obsessive compulsive disorder.)

You can't think of anything else, your world shrinks to a tiny island inhabited only by the object of your desire, and nothing else is important. It didn't help that my new beloved had just put out an album that would go platinum with four hit singles, and the song for the music video we shot together became their biggest hit. Everywhere I looked, there he was. His voice trailed me in restaurants and supermarkets, his face was on my MTV all day long.

The way Ric looked, the way he moved, was not only beautiful to me, it was also deeply familiar. Like we had already *been* in love. Yes, I had seen him on television, but there was something more to it. I just felt like I knew him already. I knew what kissing him would be like, how making love would be. It felt like coming home.

That first night, when we went to dinner at the Odeon restaurant, he was wonderful and funny in a sort of abstruse way. At one point, at my dare, he walked over to a nearby table where two people were obviously having a romantic dinner, sat right on the table, between the table settings, and just stared wordlessly at the couple. I was dying of laughter; the rest of the band looked unperturbed, and the couple was baffled. After a few minutes, he hopped off and came back to sit next to me as if nothing had happened. When he removed his nearly glued-on sunglasses, those beautiful, intense aquamarine eyes were focused only on me. The words we said, our banter that night, were inconsequential. But the way he looked at me made me feel beautiful, fully seen, and accepted.

There was a crowded nightclub, a stolen kiss in the hallway, and two days of shooting the video at a soundstage in Brooklyn, where a lot more kissing happened in my dressing room.

At some point between kisses, I asked him to tell me something secret about himself. I meant a little confidential snippet, something only I would get to know. And that's when he told me he was married. It was a glass of cold water thrown in my face. But quickly, with my nineteen-year-old reasoning, I figured it always took two to be unhappy in a relationship, so clearly his was not a good marriage. That was that. We resumed kissing.

Monday morning, only a few hours after we had finished the video, I had a shoot for American *Vogue*, to which I arrived with bleary eyes and a heart so full I could think of nothing else but him.

I LEFT MY BOYFRIEND and moved in with a girlfriend. I expected Ric to do the same. It wasn't until a few months passed of me pressing him to leave his wife that he told me there were children. Being a child of divorced parents, I could not brush this off easily. I tried to break off the relationship, but I couldn't. Instead, our love was made greater and more dramatic by the fact that it was illicit. I believed in overwhelming and endless love.

As aloof and forbidding as Ric seemed to others, he was the gentlest man when he was with me. He was very physical, very touch-oriented, and an amazing lover. At night, we'd sleep intertwined; I hardly knew where I began and he ended.

When we watched old movies together, he'd cry. Our favorite was *An Affair to Remember*. That moment when Nickie finally finds Terry in her apartment and asks why she didn't come to their meeting at the top of the Empire State Building. She won't tell him. But she keeps sitting, a blanket on her lap. Then Nickie walks into another room and sees a wheelchair up against the wall. He understands, and the look of realization on his face always made Ric break down right along with the character.

Our understanding of love was the same. Our relationship was filled with pain and beauty, and I thought that was proof of its depth. "You couldn't see the stars if it weren't for the darkness around them," Ric used to quote to me. He loved me so completely, he didn't want to share me with anyone else. I became his obsession. For the first time in my life I felt wholly desired. His insistence on the two of us always being together made me feel safe, for I believed a man who loved me this fully would never abandon me.

When he began to buy me clothes he preferred to see me in, clothing that looked very much like his—Yohji Yamamoto wide pants and black-and-white shirts—I felt embraced by his sense of style. I put aside my tight catsuits and experimental hairstyles and dressed the way he preferred. When he got jealous of my gay friends, arguing that "they would turn straight for you," I was at first reluctant to stop seeing all my gay male friends, but also weirdly flattered. Eventually I gave up all my friends, straight or gay. Nothing was as important as our love. Then it was just the two of us in his little apartment on Twelfth Street.

We watched *Star Trek* and *The Honeymooners* and made love on a green rug in front of the fireplace, unconcerned about the lack of curtains in the large picture windows. We only needed and cared about each other.

The first gift he gave me was a patterned bathrobe, like an art deco fever dream in silk, which I still own to this day. He had impeccable taste. He began buying all my clothes: baggy, geometric, architectural shirts and pants, and lots of velvets. Basically, the same way he dressed. I wanted him to find me beautiful, so I wore what he liked.

To each other, we had no flaws. No one had ever made me feel so lovable. Of course, there were many jobs he didn't want me to do, especially ones with other men. He would not share me. He flew into jealous rages often enough to make me understand how much I mattered to him. I stopped doing bookings where I had male counterparts. I stopped working weekends that were not convenient with his schedule. We made a very few select friends together, only ones who understood that we were a package. There wasn't much room for anyone else. But adoring someone takes up a lot of room. Both of our careers suffered, because we became each other's priorities.

In 1987, he left his wife. We had been living as a secret for three years. With childish naivete I never doubted our love; I believed that it was all about getting the timing right. He said he needed to wait to leave because they had young children. He had already left a set of children when he left his first wife, and he said he didn't want to do that again. I understood. And I loved him the more for it, that he was such a good father.

He told me another secret before we got married. He was actually four years older than he had initially told me—making him twenty-one years older than me. This was heartbreaking to me: he adored me so much he was insecure about his age. Of course he had lied. He didn't want to risk losing me! As if those four years made a difference in my love for him.

We married in August 1989, very shortly after his divorce was finalized. We had already bought our house in Gramercy before we married, and we lived there for the next thirty years.

I thought I had the perfect marriage.

He became my whole world, my entire universe. This was

what I always wanted, to be this important to someone. To be adored.

WHEN MY HUSBAND DIED, Griffin Dunne, our neighbor at Ric's secret apartment on Twelfth Street, immortalized a silly prank we had played on him as a story in *Vanity Fair*. Then he wrote:

> I don't think I've ever seen a couple more in love than those two. They hung on each other's words and laughed uproariously over things an outsider couldn't possibly understand. They spoke a language all their own that made you feel like you were eavesdropping on dolphins.

That was us.

UNTIL IT WASN'T. Our marriage began to dissolve as our two sons grew up. My adoration for him was subsiding, being replaced by a more clear-eyed love. I began to understand his limitations. But what he needed from me was the adoration. The blind infatuation. That was his comprehension of love. Any dissent caused him to pull away.

I construed this as turning invisible to him, gradually

receding into the wallpaper. Our means of communication and connection were physical, had always been through the body. Once he stopped wanting to touch me, I knew the relationship was doomed.

His adoration had provided a safe harbor for me for most of my life. His way to love created me. I am a woman of fifty-seven whose idea of love, until very recently, was stuck at one I developed at the age of nineteen.

I would never choose that love today. I am finally figuring out who I am and what my needs are. I'm beginning to understand that there is a lot more to me than I ever dared to explore within the confines of my marriage. I will never again sacrifice myself at the altar of love.

Even though so many years of being with my husband were wonderful, I've come to understand I'm no longer content with being an object of beauty, even if it's a precious one. I'm no longer a girl whose fear of abandonment will make her acquiesce to whatever her lover needs. I'm a woman who's lived through betrayal and grief and heartache. A woman who knows her strength. What I need and want is love. Real love. Adoration may be where love begins, like the foamy top of a beer. But love is the deeper substance underneath, the golden, effervescent beer under the foam. Adoration is overwhelming, all-consuming, and blind. Love has substance; it recognizes, acknowledges, and forgives flaws—it embraces flaws as a part of a whole, imperfect person.

In Czechia, you can order a beer without the beer; you can actually get just a glass of foam and eat it with a spoon. But it's mostly air. It will never fill you up. In hindsight, Ric and I spent so much time whipping each other up in foamy adoration, we had no time for anything else. Both of our careers suffered, we had no friends, but we were consumed with sweet clouds of bubbles. When I wanted to delve deeper, he couldn't recognize what I was offering. Ric never did appreciate the slight bitterness of beer.

KNOWING THE
FUTURE

I was seventeen and lovesick over Nigel. I couldn't stop think-ing about him: his blond curls, his dark eyes, the slant of his jaw. I had to know if I would ever see Nigel again. And that's when my friend Anne, a booker at my agency, offered me the name of a psychic.

I imagined an old woman with a crystal ball in a cluttered apartment on a dark street. Instead, I found myself walking down the majestic tree-lined Avenue Niel. The address jotted down on the scrap of paper led me to a magnificent Hauss-mannian apartment building. Its huge, perfectly symmetrical windows caught the sunlight across the smooth sand-colored stone facade. This was money. Old money. Slightly intimidated and unsure if I was in the right place, I pushed open the heavy, carved door and took the elevator to the third floor. The elevator opened to a landing with ornate, glossy wooden double doors on either side.

The tiny woman who opened the door was immaculately dressed in a pencil skirt, a silk blouse, high heels, and pearls, her hair perfectly coiffed. She looked to be in her fifties. I was about to excuse myself, saying that I must have the wrong address, when she stepped toward me, reaching up to air-kiss me. I understood then that she was the psychic.

We sat down at a table in a beautiful wood-paneled library. Almost immediately, she began to speak at length about my mother and my relationship with her. I was so bored by this that it did not occur to me to wonder how she could have known so much without asking me a thing. I just wanted to know about Nigel.

Finally, we got down to business. "What would you like to know?" she said.

I decided to play it cool. I flipped my hair back. "Um, well," I said, and pretended to be thinking. Meanwhile, my heart was pounding. "There's this man, and I'd like to know if I'll ever see him again?"

She closed her eyes briefly, leaned back, and shook her head, dismissing my question entirely with a slightly annoyed wave of her well-manicured hand. "By the time you see him again, you won't care," she said. She had just broken my heart but didn't even seem to notice. She picked up a deck of tarot cards and began to gently shuffle them. "Does your mother live in a different country?"

She went on to tell me about my career, great success, some films. "But that is not what you will really do," she told me. "You'll end up writing books."

Blah blah blah, I thought. This sounded terrible. I was going to end up an old-lady writer and I wasn't gonna be with Nigel.

"You will meet a man, famous, older," she said. "He will be married, but will get divorced for you."

I had perked up a little when she started speaking about romance, but what she was saying sounded completely unappealing. "You will be together for a long time. But it will not end . . ." She trailed off. "It will end . . ." She seemed reluctant to go on, and I didn't press because I didn't care. I was too busy mourning the fact that I was never going to embrace Nigel's slim, pale body.

ALL THE YEARS I was happily married, I never once thought to visit a psychic. When you're blissful, you have no need to know the future. You just want to be exactly where you are. But as my marriage began to stumble, my desire for clarity and reassurance about what the coming days and weeks would hold grew. I became obsessed with the Weather Channel. For about two years, I would play it on an endless loop in the kitchen. It felt better to know what to expect the next day, whether I was going to wake up to sun or rain. To be prepared. At the time, I had no idea why I was hooked on the weather, only that I needed to know what tomorrow would hold. Now I see that it was an attempt to control the unknowable future. To make sure there were no harrowing surprises lurking around the corner.

And then, when my marriage was broken beyond repair, I remembered the psychic I'd met all those years earlier in Paris. Surely there had to be an equivalent in New York City. The internet offered all sorts of healers and psychics and astrologers, but I wanted to find someone just like that woman. But what, exactly, was I seeking? I had a specific question in Paris, and I had a specific question now. I was fifty-two, had not been touched by my husband for years, and felt invisible. All I wanted to know was if I was ever going to have sex again. In hindsight, I can see I didn't just want information about getting laid. I wanted something bigger, something deeper, something I could not put my finger on, something I didn't realize at the time.

I wanted someone to give me a reason to keep going.

Tony's room was on the eleventh floor of a downtown New York office building. Although the hallway looked like any other bland office, his space had muted light, rugs, wall hangings, and candles, making it feel very cozy. Tony, a handsome man in his forties, sat behind a desk strewn with paper and crystals and tarot cards.

"You will fall in love," he said.

I laughed. I had no interest in falling in love. I was just getting out of a long marriage, and I honestly couldn't imagine ever falling in love again.

"I have no intention of falling in love," I told him confidently.

"And yet, you will." Tony smiled.

He said many other things I chose to ignore, because all I wanted was the answer to my most pressing question.

"Six to eight weeks," he said with a disarming grin.

Eight weeks later, I met the man who would become my boyfriend. The same man another psychic in Buenos Aires warned would destroy me. But neither she nor Tony told me that the heartbreak of that relationship would allow me to rebuild myself into the woman I wanted to be.

Seeing Tony was comforting. It gave me a sense of control. My future felt so uncertain, my life seemed to be disintegrating: my marriage falling apart, my children growing up and moving away, my career fading as I aged out of modeling. I had lost my sense of purpose, something that had been so steady and unwavering for decades while I was a wife and mother, but now had come to an end.

After Ric died, my desire to know the future, to feel like I had some control over events, only increased.

I grabbed at whatever flotsam drifted within my reach as I swam, direction unknown. I became hopelessly addicted to horoscopes. I subscribed to several horoscope apps that offered me daily predictions, often conflicting, and I would focus on the one I liked best. I subscribed to a daily tarot card app, which was 50 percent right. I called Tony for yearly updates. I had my birth chart done by a famous astrologer, who told me I was a battering ram made of nerve endings, the most apt description of me I've ever heard. Then I found Michelle, a woman who specialized in doing past-life regressions.

I had found her on the internet. To meet her, I rode my Vespa over to her uptown apartment in a windstorm. On the way there, I managed to get myself pulled over by a police officer, who issued me a ticket for not wearing protective eye gear. While he was writing me the ticket, I burst into tears and told him my husband had just died and I was on my way to, uh, therapy. He said, "Sorry, ma'am," and handed me the ticket.

In Michelle's sunny, beautifully decorated apartment, I lay back on a comfortable couch in her living room while she hypnotized me into a state of complete relaxation. Then, at her prompting, visuals, much like focused daydreams, began to play in my mind.

I found myself dressing for an important meeting, in what I knew to be borrowed clothing. A silver and pale blue brocade doublet and cape, matching tights, hat. I was to meet the man I hoped would be my patron, the man who would pay me for my paintings. My small attic room under the eaves had trapped the late-morning heat. Undulating shadows from the water in the canal below my building shimmered on the dusty wooden floor, my only window open to the sound of voices below. I didn't feel well. I wrote this off as excitement and anxiety about my upcoming meeting. As I left home and walked out into the street, the sun sparkled off the water, and people, so many people, crowded the narrow street. I knew I was heading for the main piazza, but sweat was pouring off me underneath the heavy brocade; I felt like I had been stuffed into a couch and forced to walk. The discomfort in my stomach kept increasing the farther I walked from my home. I felt faint from the heat and pain. And just as I was about to round a corner onto the open piazza, my bowels lost control and spilled themselves into my borrowed hose.

I found myself back in my attic room, the window wide open to air out the stink, the stink of my body unraveling. I knew I was dying. My friends, other artists, all male like me, stood at the side of my bed, looking uncertain and sad. Life was so unfair, I thought bitterly. Just when I was about to make it, I was forced to exit.

"What did you learn in this life?" Michelle asked gently.

"That life can be unfair," I said through tears. "And that I can't control the outcome."

Michelle guided me into seeing my second life, where I jumped right into dying. A mob of people surrounded me, a flurry of arms and cloth and sharp, sharp pains in my chest and stomach and back. I kept staring at the mosaic floor beneath me, cool tile in a black-and-white checkered pattern with ornamental colors woven in wreaths. At first, I wasn't sure what was happening; this was unexpected. I had come in good faith. And now I was being stabbed, over and over, still unable to believe what was going on. Once again, I was dying with the knowledge that life was unfair, this time because I had trusted the wrong people.

In the last life I visited, I was a middle-aged madam of a brothel in Paris. I had worked my way up from being a prostitute in the very same house I now owned, a tall, narrow space with a lot of stairs and red walls with gold sconces. I was not kind. I was a lonely woman with many disappointments and regrets. I was estranged from my daughter, and I took out my bitterness toward her on the young women who worked for me. But I died old, in a hospital bed surrounded by many other such beds, and my grown daughter held my hand. I cried, knowing I had not been a good mother. Yet she was there to hold my hand.

"What did you learn?" Michelle's voice was soothing, guiding me.

That nothing is more important than love.

Do I actually believe these were my past lives? Do I believe in reincarnation? Or were these "memories" really just manifestations of my subconscious mind bubbling up, trying to teach me something? Though I wish it were the former, I suspect the latter.

And yet this experience bolstered me for a little while. I felt that sense of reassurance and control I yearned for.

But why? Why would thinking about past lives give me a sense of reassurance and control over my future in this life? Because these past lives made me feel, even if only temporarily, that my present suffering had meaning. According to regression therapy, my past lives were lessons. So perhaps my present pain wasn't pointless. Perhaps it was teaching me some sort of a lesson. I was here with a purpose; my suffering had a purpose. My pain was my teacher. And that gave me hope.

When I went to visit Tony, I did so for the same reason: I needed hope. I needed to know I had a reason to keep living. Feeling desired again was the only way I could imagine escaping my crushing loneliness. I thought having sex would be the solution. So why wasn't I ecstatic at hearing I would fall in love again? Because I had loved—fully, completely—and it had brought me here, to this lonely place.

All my life I had simultaneously longed for love and been suspicious of it. I knew that I was capable of loving others, but I was not sure if it was possible for others to truly love me. I suspected I had worth. After all, my babi had loved me. So I had set out in life to find the one other person who would. I had found him, and then I had lost him.

When Tony said I would fall in love again, all I could think was *no*. I did not want to love. Love hurt. I wanted to be desired. Ric's desire for me had made me happy for years. Somehow, I rationalized that I would heal if I could get back that bubbly excitement of being adored, a feeling that Ric had lavished on me.

The desire for desire was a spark of light in the darkness. It was hope.

Perhaps predictions of the future and memories of past lives are real. Perhaps they are placebos, ways of tricking your brain into helping itself. Whether real or placebo, the result is the same. What matters is that you can find that little spark of light.

I am a big believer in placebos. It may be a sugar pill, but while dissolving on your tongue, it releases hope, one of the most effective balms in existence. In some way, I believe hope should be listed as a main biological imperative. Without it, all the other biological imperatives—territorialism, competition, reproduction—don't matter. Hope that you will be loved, that you will be heard, that you matter, that your pain has purpose, and that your life has meaning. But sometimes, the fact that tomorrow is another day is all the hope you need.

Tony sparked my hope. If he said I would fall in love, then surely it meant someone was going to fall in love with me. I would get laid. Tony had also spoken at length about my career and my children, things that ought to have been important to me, but as with the psychic in Paris, I wanted to hear only one thing. The thing that I thought would bring light in my darkness, the only light I recognized.

Hope is the biggest thing in the world and, simultaneously, the smallest. It's a source of light, but it's like capturing a firefly in a jar. It sure as hell won't light your room, but it will give you the knowledge, the understanding, that there is light in the world.

I kept relying on fireflies to light my room instead of using their faint glow to look around for better sources of light. When each firefly died, I had to catch another. And another. Hence all the psychics, astrology, past-life regressions. They didn't give me control, they didn't give me lasting reassurance, but they certainly were not a waste of time. No, they were vitally important, because they gave me renewed faith in the existence of light. My problem was my shortsightedness. I only looked for what I recognized. The firefly. But finally, one day, I understood that I needed to use the light of the firefly to look for a match that would light the candle.

Yes, I was desired by men again. But they all were just the fireflies, the sparks. Sparks, which led me to finding the candle that shed light on finding my new purpose at this stage of my life, which is what I actually needed all along. The realization that *I* am the candle.

HEIGHT

D on't diminish yourself for me," the famous actor whispered in my ear.

I had been asked to stand next to him for a photo. In my high heels and ballgown, I was a good four inches taller than him. Almost automatically, I jutted a hip and bent at my waist as I put an arm around him to meet his height.

His whisper felt like a slap. *Don't diminish yourself.* That was exactly what I was doing. I was making myself smaller to make him feel comfortable. He understood this right away, but it was the first time it was really, undeniably clear to me that I was doing this. He was right, and it was a shock.

But he had also said "for me." *Don't diminish yourself for me.* Was that true? Was I doing it for him?

I leaned closer to him and whispered back, "I'm not doing it for you. I'm doing it for myself."

When I was thirteen years old, my height became a problem. I had always been tall, but once puberty hit, I shot up to five-eleven and suddenly towered over everyone in school. My classmates nicknamed me "Giraffe" and the even-less-flattering "Moose." I skulked through the hallways at school, trying to make myself less visible, less tall. The only other girl in school my height was Kerstin, who had a permanent stoop from trying so hard. She, like me, had no dates.

How I longed to be petite. To be normal.

One night, toward the end of ninth grade, my friend Charlotte and I decided to try to sneak into a nightclub. We painstakingly applied our makeup, curled and teased our hair, and, to our amazement and delight, were let in right away by the bouncers at the door.

This was nothing like a school dance. Cigarette smoke was thick, and some strange, slightly sour stink permeated the air. It was dark, and the dance floor was packed. The disco ball reflected light like exploding shards of glass. I felt a shiver of anticipation, like a cool breeze at the height of a hot afternoon. Something vaguely but pleasantly dangerous. Things could happen here, I just knew it. Things I didn't know anything about but had heard whisperings of.

Charlotte and I moved around the club, cautiously, guiltily. She was sixteen, and I was fifteen. We had no business being inside an adult nightclub. We found seats in a corner and watched the boys on the dance floor. The men, really—they had to be over eighteen. Charlotte zeroed in on a man she liked and went to ask him to dance. I nursed my rum and Coke, trying to work up the confidence to talk to someone. Suddenly, a shadow loomed over me, blocking the lights. It was a man. Standing in front of me.

"Dance?"

I looked around to see who he was talking to before realizing it must be me. My heart dropped into my feet. He reached out his hand, and I grabbed hold of it, feeling like a Disney princess. This was really happening.

The music switched to a ballad. My favorite. "Fantasy," by Earth, Wind & Fire. This moment could not have been any more perfect.

Slowly, I stood up, ready for my life to begin on the dance floor. But as I was standing, straightening up, his head kept dipping below my eyeline. His eyes got bigger and bigger as he looked at me, and his mouth went slack. The muscles in his face released. It looked a little like he melted. We stood, holding hands across the bar table. The top of his head barely reached my shoulders. He dropped my hand, turned around, and walked back to his group of friends leaning against the bar. My almost-dance partner shook his head as he approached them. His friends laughed. He had to shout to be heard by them over the loud music, loud enough so that I heard it too: "Not sure if that's even a girl."

WHAT IS THE CONNECTION between height and femininity? As a tall woman, I can tell you that when I was younger, it was this: Height and femininity were opposites. They could not coexist. I believed that to be tall meant that you could not be feminine.

I remember seeing pictures of Dudley Moore and Susan Anton when I was thirteen or so. He came up to her shoulder. She was quite literally an entire head taller than him. Captions under the photos always commented that the only explanation for such a mismatch was that he must have been fantastic in bed. I had no idea what that meant, but I agreed. I thought, "How brave and self-confident he must be to date her, someone so much taller." It never once occurred to me to ascribe bravery and self-confidence to her in dating someone shorter than herself.

In popular photos of Prince Charles and Lady Diana in the early '80s, he towers over her. Yet, in many other photos, she wears flats, and when they're standing next to each other, they are of equal height. Clearly, the photos of him looking much taller were staged, an illusion. A man is supposed to tower over the woman he chooses to be with. It's an immediate, visible sign he is "more" than the woman.

Thirty years later, when I was helping to set up my girlfriend on a dating app and showing her how to mark off preferences—age, education, religion—we came to height. She told me she was only interested in dating men who were six feet and above. She herself is five-eight. The average height of a man in the US is five-eight, and for a woman it's five-four. But on dating apps, taller men get considerably more matches than shorter men. Just as younger women get more matches than older women. Men tend to lie about their height, while women are more inclined to lie about their age.

When I signed on to *Dancing with the Stars*, my partner was revealed on camera. I walked into the sunny white dance studio with cameras trained on my face to capture my reaction. The man who was to be my partner was standing in the middle of the room. He was ridiculously good-looking and, well, short. Shortish. Shorter than me. I didn't think much of it until we began dancing. Traditional ballroom dancing was not set up for tall women and shorter men. The traditional role of a male dancer is to lead, enfold, and balance the woman in his embrace. When he's shorter, the balance is off. One element we had to keep drilling was my backward lean. Because of the height difference between me and my partner, I had to lean much farther back than what was comfortable in order for us to maintain the "correct" form. To stay in that backward-leaning position for the entirety of the dance required me to engage every muscle in my torso and back, not something my back was at all grateful for.

I didn't realize what a strain this was until I danced with another partner on the show, a man who was taller than me. Everything fell into place. It took half the effort. It was like finding the perfect pair of jeans that fits instantly. It suddenly made sense.

The world assumes men should be taller than women.

I FOUND A MAN who was six-four to marry. At five-eleven, I was significantly shorter than Ric, and I felt absolutely feminine when I was with him. It was the first time in my life I felt delicate. I loved it.

My first boyfriend after Ric was five-seven, four inches shorter than me. At first, his size made me feel overgrown, oafish. I told all my friends I had met someone special, that he was sexy and funny and—short. I somehow felt compelled to let everyone know this. To this day, I'm not exactly sure why. But he seemed so confident that within weeks I became accustomed to our height difference and no longer saw him as short. Merely myself as overgrown.

One night we were out with our mutual friends Alex and Heidi. Alex, though short in stature, was big in personality, attitude, and confidence. He often made short jokes about himself, and that night he and I went back and forth, teasing each other in our usual fashion. Later that night, as my boyfriend and I were getting into bed, he said, "You know, you really shouldn't joke about other people's height."

I was caught off guard. I thought I had been merely joking around with Alex, not making jokes at his expense.

"Yeah," my boyfriend continued, "he may seem confident and all, but it still hurts a guy's feelings."

This is when I understood that we weren't actually talking about Alex. It was the first time my boyfriend let slip his insecurity about his height. It was also the first time I realized I wasn't the only one who was insecure about height. I had put all of my high heels into storage when my boyfriend and I started dating, not because he asked me to, but because I felt less feminine when I towered over him.

My boyfriend automatically assumed that being tall made all people confident. He'd often couch another man's misfortunes by adding, at the end, "But he is tall." He never said that about a woman. Being tall as a woman is not a privilege, the way it is for a man, except, perhaps, if you're a model.

My six-five son has, over the course of his life so far, gotten so many of the same comments about his height that he has his retorts ready to go. Some of them are borrowed from his six-four father. To "You play basketball?" he'll retort, "Do you play mini golf?" You can make fun of a tall man, but his very essence, his masculinity, will never be questioned. When you make fun of a tall woman, you're doing exactly the opposite. By being tall, she has inadvertently stepped into the male domain.

Short boys in school often become smart or funny or athletic to build themselves up. The operative term here is to "build up." Tall girls have to lessen themselves, be less of everything.

WHEN I BECAME a fashion model at fifteen, my height was a professional asset. And so, I could stand tall when I worked. But off the set, I would still stoop, as was my habit. It wasn't until I met Eva, also a model, that I found a different perspective. She was six feet tall, a Swedish Amazon. She was six years older than me, already established in the world of modeling, and I thought she was beyond cool. She'd wear black high-heeled boots with her faded denim jeans, a black biker's jacket, and no makeup when she was off the job. She carried her height like a torch. Standing next to her, I felt more petite, the way I thought other girls must feel. It was what I imagined "normal" felt like.

But this is where I realized something unexpected: when I felt "normal," as I felt standing next to Eva, I also felt less powerful. Being in her shadow diminished my own sense of power. It was only by feeling shorter that I understood the power of height. Tall women were powerful women. And only drew the men who were up to the challenge.

When we see photos of men and women together, where the man is shorter than the woman, we often automatically give credit to the man. He must be so confident. He must be great in bed. He must be powerful or rich or famous. No one appreciates the self-confidence of the taller woman.

"Don't diminish yourself for me." The words of a confident man. One who allows you to claim your space. But also one who assumes you're doing something *for him*.

After my relationship with my first boyfriend after Ric ended, I asked a man I was dating whether he thought I was intimidating. He answered: "Hell yeah." He listed my fabulous qualities and ended with, "And you're tall." By mentioning my height along with my great qualities, he made it seem like a rather wonderful thing.

My high heels came out of storage.

For my twelfth birthday I asked for a Mr. Spock doll. *Star Trek* was my favorite TV program, and I had developed a total crush on Mr. Spock. My mom got me my coveted Mr. Spock doll and threw in a Captain Kirk doll as well. I was so excited. My Barbies would finally have proper boyfriends. But when I unwrapped the packages and introduced them to my Barbies, the scale was off. Mr. Spock and Captain Kirk came up to my Barbies' boobs. Going out on the town would be very awkward. But I discovered that when I put them in bed together and pulled up the covers, the height difference ceased to be an issue. In my fifties, I finally confirmed through experience that this was true. There is no height difference in bed.

So why did I stoop with the Hollywood actor? Was I really doing it for myself?

Well, I certainly wasn't doing it for him. But I was trying to diminish myself. Visually, in order to be "feminine," our culture tells women we need to be smaller. And it tells us we need to diminish ourselves in other ways. But pretending to be less rich or less smart or less successful or less powerful doesn't show in pictures.

When I first began dating my shorter boyfriend, bending down to kiss was distracting. After spending most of my life with a man significantly taller than myself, where I could always be Scarlett O'Hara, now I felt more like Shrek, towering over him. It didn't render him less sexy. But it made *me* feel less sexy. Yet it took only a month for me to get used to this new way of kissing, and I realized, as I stooped over for a beautiful, passionate kiss, I was not an ogre, but a weeping willow tree, gently bowing over my partner, a gesture of trust and giving. I could both stand tall and be strong, but also be flexible when the occasion called for it. I was feminine in my flexibility, height be damned. Or celebrated.

MAGICAL MONEY

My mom was losing her mind. She announced it one day at the kitchen table in our new apartment. She told me she was going to Italy for two weeks to reclaim her sanity.

"Your dad will take care of you," she said, packing her bags.

Our dad had never been left in charge of us for more than a weekend, so I absorbed the news with a little trepidation. We had been in Sweden for only three months at this point, and he had already moved out. He now lived in another town, about twenty minutes away by car, with his new girlfriend.

Even at nine years old, I understood why my mom needed to go away. She had been crying and lashing out a lot. My dad came the afternoon after she left, sat with me for a while, and gave me a hundred kronor, the equivalent of about twenty dollars.

That was the last I saw of him until my mother returned. Looking back, there had clearly been some sort of miscommunication between my parents. But since I didn't have my mother's telephone number in Italy and didn't want to bother my dad, a man I barely knew, I was on my own. I was going to run the household for two weeks with my three-year-old brother and a hundred kronor.

Fortunately, my brother went to daycare at the home of a lovely woman named Inga, who took care of three other toddlers. So all I had to do was give him breakfast, take him to Inga's apartment before I went to school, pick him up at five, give him dinner, get him ready for bed, and put him to sleep. Then I'd do my incomprehensible Swedish school homework. With the hundred kronor, I bought white bread, spreadable cheese, milk, eggs, and toilet paper from the supermarket downstairs. We had bread with cheese for breakfast each morning, and at night I made pancakes. But a week later, we ran out of food. There was only one way I could think of to get more.

May in Sweden is still fairly cold, so my windbreaker wouldn't seem out of place. After getting home from school, I put on the windbreaker, zipped it up to my neck, and went downstairs to the dark little supermarket. Our elderly neighbor was perusing canned soups, and a bored store clerk was reading a magazine at the register. I made my way over to the refrigerated aisle. A carton of milk was too heavy and bulky, but the prepackaged spreadable cheese—the same kind I had

chosen so carefully the week before, to maximize my funds—
would be easy. I grabbed it, pretending to read the ingredients
as I looked around to make sure there was no one watching,
and then I slipped it into my jacket. Instantly, I felt like I had
been coated in a layer of neon paint that marked me as a thief
and a criminal. My heart hammered, and I had trouble catching my breath. I pushed myself to walk to the bakery section,
waiting for the woman with a shopping basket to make her
selections while I pretended to study my choices. As soon as
she walked away, I grabbed the first thing in front of me, prepackaged sliced white bread, and stuffed it into my jacket along
with the cheese. My windbreaker was fortuitously balloon-like
and cinched at the hips, so my two items were somewhat hidden, especially when I put my hands in my pockets. While my
hands were in my pockets, I squashed the bread flatter and
tried to casually saunter to the door. The store clerk looked up
at me, and I realized I couldn't just walk out. A kid in a giant
windbreaker who buys nothing is too obvious. I went to the
counter and quickly selected the cheapest thing I could find—
a pack of Wrigley's gum—and fished out some change from
my pocket. I could feel sweat gather coldly in the T-shirt fabric under my arms. I couldn't look the store clerk in the eyes.

I was certain that he would see that I was a thief. He would
grab me, unzip my jacket, and my world as I knew it would
end. Of course, I couldn't deny stealing if I was caught red-
handed. While he counted the change, I was already envision-

ing myself being taken away in a police car, worrying about who would collect my little brother from Inga at five, being interrogated under hot lights by cops who'd maybe offer me a cup of cold black coffee.

But the clerk took my change and I walked out. Into freedom. I took a giant gulp of the rainy air and tried to suppress my urge to run the few steps to our front door. A police siren flared from far away. This was it. They were coming for me. I ran, pulling open the glass door to our apartment building and hurtling up the stairs. I rushed into the apartment, hid the bread and the cheese under the seat cushion of our mustard pleather couch, and sat down at the table in the kitchen, shaking. I continued shaking long after the sound of the siren had dwindled away. I had gotten away with my crime. But for the next thirty years or so, a police siren always made my heart drop. I always felt, for a brief moment, that they were coming for me. Not for the theft of bread and cheese. No, for thirty years, a police siren was a reminder that I was a bad person, a criminal at heart. A reminder that I was a person who did not actually belong, an outcast. I had been getting away with it. I had fooled the world into thinking I was a supermodel, when in fact I was a petty thief.

I BEGAN TO MAKE my own money the next year, at the age of ten, when I found a job selling the Swedish newspaper *Kvälls-*

posten. A big bundle of newspapers was left on our doorstep every day, and after school I would go and sell them in our housing project. I would stuff as many copies as I could carry into a satchel that I slung over my shoulder, and then I'd go ring doorbells and knock on doors. Each opened door gave me a peek into someone else's life. Swedish lives. Apartments were furnished simply with plain, boxy IKEA furniture and smelled of summer sausage and lingonberries. It was a stark difference from the homes in Czechoslovakia I'd grown up with, where everyone hung lace curtains on the windows, furniture was scuffed and well used, and the hallways always smelled of boiled cabbage, roast pork, and furniture polish. Some of my customers seemed lonely, the apartments behind them dark and sad. They would chat for a minute or two before handing me my money. Others just pushed the money at me and slammed the door. I discovered that if I brought along my four-year-old brother, business improved. I'd knock, stick the paper into his hands, and push him forward.

"Kvällsposten!" he announced, very seriously, in his trembly baby voice. Very few people had the heart to refuse. And when they did, my little brother would burst into tears, cinching the sale.

I rarely made more than thirty kronor, about five dollars a week, but that was enough to purchase candy at our local candy store, where all the other kids went. After a year, my brother refused to go with me, my sales fell, and I gave up.

Instead, I babysat for the woman in the apartment above us. The first time I babysat for her, she told me she had full confidence in me after watching how I took care of my brother, and left me with her six-month-old baby for the evening. I was told to brush his teeth after giving him his bottle. All went well until I coated his toothbrush with toothpaste and stuck it in his mouth. All hell broke loose. The baby wouldn't stop screaming. I ran next door to my best friend Malin's apartment with the baby in my arms, where Malin's mom explained the baby wasn't used to minty-fresh toothpaste, washed out its screaming pink mouth, and handed it back to me. The baby's mom was none the wiser, but I was; I never attempted to brush that baby's teeth again.

BY THE TIME I was thirteen, I became convinced that the reason I wasn't "normal" like the other kids at school was that I didn't have the money to purchase their trendy jeans and lip gloss. I wore secondhand clothing my mom got from a thrift store: pants that were flared and always too short, bohemian sweaters and blouses that were popular in the late '60s and '70s but which now looked tragically out-of-date against the skin-tight jeans and crop tops of the early '80s.

I was certain that my clothes were the reason I was bullied by the meanest girl in school, Aneka, and her two hench-women I ungraciously thought of as Humpty and Dumpty.

Aneka was always well dressed. She wore skintight pegged jeans and short-sleeved shirts, which she tied at the waist. She curled her hair out into wings and lined her eyes with baby-blue sparkly pencil. Humpty and Dumpty, one brunette, one blonde, were always dressed in denim ensembles that were just a bit too snug to look comfortable. Every time they passed me in the hallway, they'd shout, "Dirty Communist!"

Skulking through the school hallways, afraid of my shadow, I bemoaned my freakish height and my secondhand clothes. It was my clothes that made me different, I told myself. While I couldn't change my height, I could change my clothes. But I could do that only if I had money.

IN THE LAST MONTH of eighth grade, I began to work at a clothing store that specialized in selling dresses to older women. Frumpy, I thought. Bow ties and muted colors. At fourteen, I thought anyone who was past thirty seemed "older." I managed to sell one dress all by myself to a grandmother, who told my colleagues I was fabulous and my enthusiasm had made her purchase the dress. The job was boring, most of the time the store was empty, but my colleagues—two "older" women—were friendly. We drank a lot of black coffee and listened to Barry Manilow. Most importantly, the money I made was all mine. I could finally buy the stonewashed jeans I had been coveting, the ones I believed would change my life.

I started the first day of ninth grade filled with hope, dressed in an outfit I had spent all summer planning. I wore my new pair of tight stonewashed jeans, a yellow T-shirt with cherries printed across my chest, and black Converse sneakers. I had a tan from the summer, and I had flipped my new Dorothy Hamill haircut into the obligatory side wings, lined my eyes with blue, and applied Bonne Bell strawberry lip gloss. I was ready to be normal.

I walked down the school hallway, feeling different. I met my classmates' eyes as I passed them and smiled, tossing my wings. But instead of being shocked by my transformation, their faces remained blank. No smiles were returned. I was still invisible. I went to my new locker, dropped off some books, picked up what I needed for geography, and went to class. Somehow, despite all the effort I had put in, I was still inconsequential, a fart in the wind. Suddenly my new clothes felt stiff and restrictive. Like I had showed up to a party dressed in a costume while everyone else was in regular clothes. I felt not just invisible, but pathetic.

But during the lunch break, as I passed Aneka and her henchwomen on my way to my locker, I finally got the reaction I was hoping for. Their eyes went wide; their mouths dropped open a little.

"Well, fuck me," Aneka exhaled.

Pleased, I pulled my books from my locker with a smile. I decided to make a quick trip to the bathroom on the lower floor before I headed upstairs for class. As usual, it was deserted—it was why I always picked this bathroom. As I flushed, I heard the door open and footsteps follow. I walked out of the stall to go to the sinks. Aneka and her friends were waiting for me.

"Well, hello there," she said.

I smiled at her. My transformation was working. "Hi, guys."

"Nice new look."

I was about to thank her when she narrowed her eyes. "For a hooker," she hissed.

Slightly disoriented, I wondered to myself if that could be a compliment. I supposed some hookers did have elements of glamour about them, right? Like courtesans in Paris . . .

"I think you need to take a shower, whore," Aneka said. Humpty and Dumpty grabbed me by the arms. Okay, it wasn't a compliment.

I didn't exactly understand what was happening, even as it happened. They pushed me back into the stall and forced me to my knees.

"Dirty whore," Aneka said, grabbing me by the back of my neck and pushing my head into the toilet bowl.

"Dirty whore, dirty whore, dirty whore," Humpty and Dumpty chanted as Aneka flushed.

Cold water hit my scalp and then rushed into my nose. I couldn't breathe. I swallowed water. Toilet water, I realized, and gagged. The pressure of their hands lessened, and I pulled my head out to breathe. Coughing, eyes stinging, nose burning, with water running down my hair and neck and onto my new T-shirt, I sat back on my heels and cried. I could hear Aneka and her friends laughing as they walked out the door.

Eventually I made my way to class, late, my hair still damp.

After that incident, I understood that I couldn't buy my way out of being just, somehow, wrong. Flawed. Bad.

Money didn't save me. It made things worse.

HAVING MONEY does save you from some very real things.

It saves you from starving. It saves you from having to steal food. It saves you from getting arrested for stealing food.

At some point between the day I stole bread and cheese and the first day of ninth grade, I had begun seeing money as almost magical. I believed it would save me from everything that caused me pain. It was the solution to everything, I thought. And it was attainable. It wasn't like my wish to be a foot shorter, which could never come true. If I worked hard enough, I could make enough money to buy myself out of my pain. I could buy the things that would fix me. I could buy all the things I longed for: bread, cheese, pancake mix, tight jeans, crop tops, acceptance, love.

The best thing about my belief in the magic of money was the hope it offered. I could taste the possibility of fitting in. It was so close. That summer I worked in the clothing shop, as I saved my kronors and coins, I was lifted up, buoyed by the faith that the money I earned would allow me to buy the new clothes that would save me. The most painful thing about the first day of ninth grade was not the bullying, the humiliation. It was the loss of hope—the shattering of the belief that money was an achievable kind of magic.

THE RESPONSIBILITY
OF BEAUTY

Easy for you to complain about the system now
that you aren't an "it" girl—but you had no
problem making millions of dollars, enjoying your
celebrity, and making millions of young girls feel
ugly and unworthy for decades. NOW you are
aware of how fragile self-image is???? You played
a big role in creating the machine that makes
people feel worthless if they aren't "magazine
beautiful," and now you are crying because the
system is making you feel like you made everyone
else feel. The hypocrisy is incredible.

This was a comment I received on Instagram a little while
ago. I've heard variations of this comment ever since I first
became a model. When I was twenty and had just signed on

with Estée Lauder, I was interviewed by a journalist who asked me what I thought the responsibility of beauty was. I was totally stumped by her question.

She tapped her pen on her notepad, clarifying. "For example, would you sell furs? Or, say, blood diamonds?"

Her question made me feel defensive. It seemed like she assumed that there was a responsibility to beauty—that beauty was a gift to be used virtuously, for moral good. But does being beautiful mean that you have a greater responsibility to be virtuous? By that same logic, would someone less beautiful have less responsibility to be virtuous?

But the truth was that her question also shamed me. I had become a model at fifteen and made a great deal of money because people thought I was beautiful. I was also an arrogant asshole. Give a teenager loads of money, no rules, and lavish praise for her ability to look stunning and fit into sample-size clothing, and moral responsibility probably isn't what she spends most of her days thinking about.

Nevertheless, her question stuck with me for the following thirty-some years. What is the responsibility of beauty? What is the responsibility of someone who has been given the gift of beauty? Is it to use that beauty to do good in the world? Is it to try to preserve and maintain that beauty, the way we'd maintain an eighteenth-century Stradivarius violin? The question sat there, haunting me. I had no answer but I continually puzzled over it.

———

WHEN YOU BUY ART, you want it to remain the same. If you buy Van Gogh's *Sunflowers*, you don't want to wake up one morning and discover it has changed to *Tulips*. When beauty is captured in a piece of art, we strive to maintain it. Museums, art galleries, and patrons of the arts spend incredible resources on curating environments with perfect lighting, temperature, and humidity to allow their art to remain unchanged. So, is the responsibility of beauty to just self-preserve?

Certainly, my responsibility as a model was to *not change*, to be a prototype of the ideal woman. The perfect canvas. Blemishes, bloodshot eyes, scars, too much weight, or hair in the wrong places—all were my responsibility *not* to have. They were blemishes, something to fix. Like wrinkles and softer, draping skin. So, it seemed my responsibility—the responsibility of beauty—was indeed just to remain beautiful to uphold a beauty standard set by mainstream society.

People seem to understand that being beautiful is neither an accomplishment nor a fault. It is a gift. Generally, if you are given a gift or something of great value, your responsibility is to make use of it. When a person is born with an athletic or artistic ability and becomes a celebrated athlete or artist, we don't shame them for using their gift. If a child is intelligent, we encourage them to get an education, to study hard, to develop their gift of intelligence as much as possible, and then use that gift out in the world. Developing their gift is seen as their responsibility. Wasted talent is a waste of potential. But when your gift is beauty, developing it is considered vain and narcissistic. Trying to maintain it is likewise shameful, whereas in athletics it's practically heroic. An older athlete who strives to maintain their athleticism and compete with younger athletes is regarded as brave. An older model who strives to maintain their beauty and compete with younger models is often regarded as unnatural, embarrassing.

Also, somewhere along the way, we pick up the message that we can't be beautiful *and* intelligent. That if we want to be taken seriously for our intelligence, we have to downplay our beauty. Right before I moved to Paris, I thought of myself as ugly and smart. Once I started working as a model, I was suddenly beautiful and stupid. When I called my dad to tell him I was staying in Paris to model full-time, he said, "Oh, now you're going to be a dumbass." When I arrived in Paris I got a reading list from a university and decided to read all the books listed in the English literature syllabus, not because I necessarily liked them or would choose them on my own, but because I wanted to make sure people knew I was intelligent.

THOUGH BEAUTY may be seen as a gift, beauty is also ambiguous and contradictory. It is subjective. What I may find beautiful may not be the same as what you find beautiful. The perception of beauty changes. Just in the past few decades, we have gone from celebrating the '80s glamazon to the '90s waifs to the 2000s enhanced curves.

Being seen as beautiful is all about being in the right place at the right time with the right attributes. Had you plunked me down a century earlier, I would have been a sallow, forbiddingly tall, and angular woman with few marriageable prospects. After all, Van Gogh had died penniless, unable to sell much of his art.

I had an inkling of the fleetingness and changeability of physical beauty, because I knew what it felt like to be regarded as ugly. I had been ugly in school, mercilessly bullied by pretty blondes. When I arrived in Paris to model, I was called beautiful for the very same features that had made me ugly in Sweden. I'd stare at my face in the mirror, the one that had been considered homely in one country and attractive in another. But I had not changed. I started to get an inkling that it may not actually be about me, but the onlookers.

I was once asked, in a writing workshop, to write two paragraphs on the same object of beauty. One from the perspective of a person who had just fallen in love, the other from the perspective of someone who was heartbroken. I picked a rose. As someone who had just fallen in love, the rose was intoxicating. I wrote about every lovely detail: the dew collected on the petals, the colors of a sunset swirled into the bloom, the scent that made me leap back in time to when my lover had presented me with a single one to say he loved me. I imbued the rose with all the hope I felt, and it became the most beautiful thing in the world. As someone heartbroken, I took notice of its thorns, how they jutted out to hurt me. The beauty of the bloom was an insult, a reminder of all I had lost. The rose hadn't changed. But how I perceived it did.

I STRUGGLED WITH SHAME across my forty-plus-year career as a model. While a woman seeing a photo of me in an ad might have felt shame for not looking like me, I had been shamed for not having the body of Elle Macpherson. And the boobs of Cindy Crawford. And the teeth of Christie Brinkley. When the standard you are being held to is physical perfection, none of us can compete. I just quietly envied those other models and decided I surely had other, more important attributes. I was smarter, I could play the piano and draw, and I was certain I read way more books. I cut other women down in my mind so I could feel, if not superior, at least equal. I turned around and shamed those women after feeling shamed myself.

In my experience, no one shames a woman as often and as effectively as other women. We are all in the same boat, wanting to go the same way, yet instead of working together to get there, we knock one another off the boat. Do we not understand that the fewer of us there are to paddle, the slower we advance?

Who wins the race when we're so busy knocking one another down? Most likely the very people and systems who set the race up in the first place. Who benefits from our insecurities of being too fat, too hairy, too dark, too old? The companies that make money selling us the products to "fix" it all. I contributed to the system, the one that set up the race by selling those very products. I had done so by accepting and using the gift I had been given.

Being in possession of beauty is a privilege. There is undeniable power in it. In general, the world responds more positively to beauty—doors might open a little faster, a little wider. Choosing to engage in the maintenance or manufacture of beauty—choosing to wear makeup, or dye your hair, or wear fashionable clothes—these are things we choose to do to access a little of that privilege. But it's not our responsibility to be beautiful. It's a gift we give ourselves since our society celebrates it. And if we are born with the right attributes, at the right time, and in the right place to be called beautiful, we are not responsible for the gifts handed to us. But we are responsible for how we use them.

Today, being a mature woman, I would not choose to sell blood diamonds or furs. I'm annoyed when women try to sell me creams that they claim restored their face to prepubescence when it's obvious a talented doctor had something to do with it. On my Instagram page, I'm scrupulously honest about the things I use and don't use, because I want to use the privileges

I have responsibly. But I am a woman now, not a child, not a "girl." I have had decades to think about the question I was asked so many years ago.

As for the person who left that comment for me on Instagram—she's not only shaming me for being beautiful, for making her feel inadequate, but also for using the privileges bestowed on me because of it. But if she has ever bought a moisturizer or a lipstick or even a magazine, she has played a part in conferring that privilege upon me. This is just how this system works. We both perpetuate it by participating.

We often try to capture beauty when we see it. We try to make that perfect, beautiful moment live on forever by putting it in song, or on canvas, or in dance. We create art so we can trap a fleeting feeling of joy that seeing beauty produces in us.

We try to own beauty, but it cannot be owned. Beauty is like love in that way. It is a feeling, not an object. It's an adjective, not a noun. Beauty is not responsible for your reaction to it. You are responsible for your own reactions when experiencing beauty.

The responsibility of beauty is not in the beheld; it's in the eye of the beholder.

FAME

When the phone rang in my little studio apartment early in the morning on a Saturday, I was surprised. No one ever called me on weekend mornings. I rolled out of the pale pink sheets (which I needed to wash, as soon as I could figure out where the laundromat was) and padded over to the beige rotary phone at the far end of the room. One wall of my studio apartment in Paris was lined with tall windows that looked out onto a concrete backyard, but the other three walls were bizarrely covered in dark blue padded fabric. The brown corduroy couches that came with the place didn't exactly brighten things up. I had walked into a rental office all by myself and agreed to take the very first apartment they showed me. I was sixteen and had no idea I could refuse and look at other apartments.

The phone kept ringing. The agency was closed over the weekend, and all my friends would still be sleeping off last night's party. I picked it up with hesitation. The voice on the other end sounded male. It sounded faraway.

"Hi, this is Joe."

I quickly went through my internal Rolodex but couldn't come up with a Joe. My silence prompted a quick follow-up. "You don't know me, but . . ."

Ah, I didn't know him. Before I could wonder why he was calling me, he continued.

"I saw you in *Sports Illustrated*, and I think you're so beautiful, and I have a prom coming up so I wondered maybe, if you could, um, if I could, like, take you as my date?"

I was speechless. My photo, just my photo, had led someone—a stranger—to track down my phone number and call me.

This was the first time I felt famous.

"Oh my God, this is so nice! That's so sweet of you! What's a prom?"

He explained it was the end-of-the-year dance for his high school.

"That sounds fun! Okay!"

"So, I go to Topeka High. It's on May twenty-sixth, at seven. The dance is in the gym, but I figure I could take you out to dinner beforehand. What kind of food do you like?"

"I like everything, honestly."

"Okay, then we'll go out for burgers. You like burgers? I know the best place to go."

"Sure, burgers sound good. What should I wear? What do people wear to proms?"

"The girls usually wear, like, fancy long dresses. Like with ruffles and bows."

Almost forty years later, writing this essay, I googled 1983 vintage prom dresses to remind myself what they looked like. The first picture that popped up, of three girls in maroon taffeta and white lace ruffled dresses with giant puffed sleeves and princess waists, were three girls I knew from my modeling days: Eva, Marilyn, and Dawn. By the time I made it to the US at seventeen, I had already "aged out" of modeling the glory that was the '80s prom dress, thank goodness.

"Okay, I'll figure something out . . ."

"So I could pick you up at five, so we have plenty of time. Where will you be?"

"Uh, well, I'm in Paris."

"Oh, right," he said slowly. "So, can you come here? To Kansas?"

"Um. Huh." And it was only then that it dawned on me that there was no way I could make it to his prom, as much as I may have wanted to please Joe. He was my first fan. My first taste of being important to somebody, even if he was somebody I didn't know. Feeling important was something that felt deliciously novel, something utterly unexpected. It was a strange warmth.

Just a few months later I would move to the US, and I would have to have an unlisted phone number because there were a lot of Joes who wanted to take me out. Eventually I would even have to change my name on hotel bookings, have a bodyguard follow me during personal appearances, and put all my bills in assumed names.

But at first, before all that happened, being famous was intoxicating.

I had been famous, to some extent, most of my life. As a child, I was famous in Sweden, but at the time I lived in Czechoslovakia, so I had no idea that I was famous—or even what being famous meant. After I moved to Sweden, I discovered that being known as a political refugee was more infamy than fame. It was being constantly pitied, condescended to, and patronized; receiving a pat on the head for being "poor little Paulina," saved by the Swedish. I was famous because I was pathetic. It may have gotten me some compassion from adults, but it repulsed my schoolmates. They saw me as weak and treated me like I trailed a bad smell.

But this new sort of fame—fame for being considered beautiful—felt, at first, like love. Suddenly people approved of me. They wanted to be my friends. They wanted more of me. It took me years to understand that their attention was not love.

Fame

To be famous is to be in a bubble. The outer surface of the bubble is reflective, mirrored. It means that when people look at someone famous, they don't actually see the person inside the bubble—they see themselves. We assume that being famous means everybody knows you. But in fact, being famous means nobody knows you. Instead, people project their own assumptions, ideas, and desires onto you, and the real you is lost to their illusions of who they want you to be. It's why they won't ever know you.

As a child who had been abandoned by her mother, I longed for my mother's approval and love. I wanted her—and, by extension, everyone I met—to know me and to accept me. But fame made that feel almost impossible. It ensured that I would rarely be seen or loved for who I am, more often for what I represented to whoever was looking at me. It created a barrier around me during the very years I most needed to be accepted for who I was as a person.

Fame doesn't just prevent people from knowing you; it also walls you off. It prevents you from connecting with other people. This is what I wanted as a child and as a teenager, what I have always wanted. To connect. To be seen and heard for who I am and not who you want me to be. But fame replaces connections with assumptions. When people approach you with assumptions of who you are, you will inevitably fail to live up to those assumptions.

Being famous as a model, I became one-dimensional—a

blank page, a paper doll. Most people never heard me speak; all they knew of me was my face and body, onto which they could project anything they wanted.

THEN SOMETHING SHIFTED. Once I made my first *Sports Illustrated* bathing suit cover, I was asked to do interviews. To the public, I began to have more of a voice and a personality. And to my surprise, I was sometimes disliked. I had no idea that hearing me speak would shatter some peoples' notions of who I was.

I just answered all questions honestly. I noticed that people wanted to know more about me. What I ate for breakfast and what TV shows I watched. This heightened my sense of self-importance but did nothing for my self-confidence. I became simultaneously more arrogant and less secure. I knew that I was being celebrated for something I was not—and this just made me more fearful that I would be found out; that people would discover that I wasn't actually beautiful, that I was still just "poor little Paulina." This all happened so gradually that I didn't realize what was happening until it had already happened.

It was around this time that I met Ric. When two famous people meet, the bubbles around them can easily merge, just like real soap bubbles. I think this is why famous people often hang out with other famous people. You can connect with that person right way. It's almost like being an American living in a foreign country. You're surrounded by people who eat, who sleep, who dream like you, but the moment you spot another American, you're instantly sucked into a bubble of shared commonalities.

There is an assumption that being famous means that life is more comfortable. And it's true that fame often comes with wealth, and wealth does indeed make life comfortable. But the more famous you are, the more constricted your life also becomes. It's as though the more famous you are, the smaller that bubble around you gets. Ric had a much smaller bubble than me. When I was alone, I could do things that Ric could never do, like go grocery shopping or take the kids to school without being accosted. But when we were together, I was drawn into his tiny bubble. He had been living in his small bubble for a long time, and it suited him perfectly.

The deep problems with existing within the fame bubble only really became clear to me when I began dating in my fifties. My husband had died, my boyfriend had left me, and my children had moved out. I was desperately alone, and not at all accustomed to it. When I complained about the lack of available men, I was told to go for *real* people, *real* guys. In other words, not famous. I ended up at dinners with doctors and lawyers and real estate developers and bankers. The result was always the same. They were so consumed with staring at themselves in the reflection of my bubble, it was impossible to connect.

My first task at the beginning of any date was to try to puncture the bubble and humanize myself. To allow them to see *me*, not their idea of me. I knew that this was best accomplished by presenting myself as flawed and vulnerable. And goofy, which I am by nature. I usually ended up expending so much energy on this that I never even got to flirt.

Occasionally, I will encounter someone who is aware of the existence of the bubble, and who thinks that they can puncture the bubble by force. They are the people who will walk up to you and, instead of asking for an autograph, tell you what they think is wrong with you. But while these barbed comments can sometimes sting, they don't burst the bubble— ultimately, it's clear that the insults are, like the compliments, just the other person projecting their inner world onto you.

So what removes the bubble? The only thing that can destroy it is indifference. When everyone ignores the person inside the bubble, the bubble will slowly disintegrate. Gradually. So gradually the person inside won't even notice until it's gone.

The reason, I believe, why people think fame is desirable is because fame comes with the illusion of being heard. We all want to be heard. With fame, your voice is amplified. But like a megaphone, fame can also distort as it amplifies.

I've been famous for most of my life. Sometimes less, sometimes more. I suppose if I left everything I know and love and moved to a hut in Siberia, I could be unfamous. But then I'd also be completely isolated. So my choice is between sitting in my bubble with my really nice wallpaper and ignoring the outside world, which I can see but not touch, or using the megaphone I have been given. I'd rather be lonely with a purpose than lonely without a purpose.

Since I have the amplified voice of fame, I can use it to talk about things that matter to me. I can use it to speak to you.

GRIEF AND
BETRAYAL

My brother walked up behind me as I was standing by the kitchen sink in the house upstate. It was September, but it still felt like summer. The windows were all open, the air was warm and still. About forty people mingled throughout the house. I felt like I was in a train station surrounded not by friends and family, but by strangers. I was gripping the porcelain double sink, original to this old house in the country, relying on it to hold myself up. The walls were bright yellow. I had painted and glazed them myself while six months pregnant with our second son, Oliver. Ric and I had bought this house when Jonathan was three and "made" Ollie there when the house still had no furniture. There was a pot in front of me. I wasn't quite sure what to do with it. Did I mean to cook something or wash it? I stared out the window at the trees. They were still green.

"Hey, sis," my brother said.

He startled me, but I barely reacted. If he had come at me brandishing a frying pan I would have had the same reaction. I had zero instinct for self-preservation, zero ability to make choices.

"What the hell was Ric thinking?"

"I hope he was thinking about the cookies," I said.

My brother looked baffled. "Cookies?

"Yeah," I said. "I got him cookies. From this place. You know, a cookie place. The fresh-baked cookie place. You know, those cookies."

I had gone out the night before for a friend's birthday, making sure Ric was all set at home with the boys, and on the way back I got him some chocolate chip cookies from one of those little hole-in-the-wall, open-late places. But he said he wasn't in the mood for them when I got home and asked me to save them for the next day.

I leaned against the sink, the pot forgotten. "So, I gave him a kiss goodnight, and that's the last time . . ." I began sobbing.

My brother watched me for a while. "I was talking about the will," he said quietly.

The will. Oh yes, the will.

It bobbed like an unexploded mine in the black water we were treading.

I HAD BEEN TOLD of my husband's last wishes the day after his death by his best friend and manager, Jeff. But indirectly. Mysteriously. We were talking on the phone about the funeral. Jeff and his wife were going to fly to LaGuardia in two days; they would stay at a hotel in the city and would drive up to Millbrook for the funeral.

Then, suddenly, mid-sentence about renting a car, Jeff blurted out, "You'll be fine, don't worry, you'll be fine."

I briefly wondered why he sounded so insistent, so apologetic.

"You'll get both of the houses and the pension plan. It'll be fine."

I didn't know why he was telling me this.

"I had to set up the trust for the boys. That just had to be done."

"Okay," I replied, confused. "A trust sounds good."

I couldn't hold on to any real thoughts. I had no idea what he was talking about, and no capability to inquire.

A few days later, while we were still in the city before the funeral, three large gray envelopes appeared. They had materialized on the table that we piled mail on, the little table that

Ric and Ollie had found on the street and lugged home. One envelope for me and one for each of our boys. I don't know if they had been delivered by messenger or mail or UPS, or who brought them into the house. The envelopes contained Ric's will.

> *I will make no provisions for my wife*
> *because she abandoned me.*

"She abandoned me." *Abandoned.* I kept reading the words over and over. It felt like I was falling.

This was a mistake. Someone had made a mistake. Surely I would get a phone call, someone would contact me to clarify. Ric had not said that. I had clearly not abandoned him. Though we had separated, we remained best friends. We still lived together. Perhaps he had said it in anger, someone had jotted it down, and it had accidentally ended up in the will. This was a draft, this was someone's notes. These were not his last wishes. This was some sort of terrible fuckup at the lawyer's office.

So I put it aside, this mistake. It simply did not penetrate my brain.

Jeff showed up the next day at the house. He helped me pick out clothes for Ric to wear in his casket. I thought it should be a comfy outfit he would've worn at home, not a suit. I wanted him to be cozy and comfortable. We cried but also had a few laughs as Jeff and his wife sat on our bed and I went through Ric's closet—and our shared histories—holding up items of clothing, memories to consider. It was such an intimate moment, dressing my husband for forever.

We did not talk about the will.

When my brother approached me at the kitchen window after the funeral, Jeff was one of the people milling around in the house. I still had not made the connection between what Jeff said on the phone and the reality of what the will meant. What it meant for me, for my sons, for our entire family.

CAN YOU HOLD ON TO two disparate emotions at the same time? Sure. We are complex beings. You can be delighted that you found a dream house that is within your price range, and at the same time be upset that the reason it's within your price range is because a murder was committed in the front hallway. You can be mad at your husband for forgetting the dry cleaning when you really needed that cocktail dress tonight, but also be delighted by the bouquet of flowers he brought you instead. Happy/sad. Pleased/angry. Our contrasting emotions are two ends of a seesaw, and the seesaw wobbles back and forth. Hopefully we find a peaceful balance in the middle.

Grief and betrayal are separate emotions, but they are on the same side of the seesaw. The terrible side. There is no balance.

Experiencing both at the same time is like experiencing a

really bad case of food poisoning. The poison inside you has to come out, and just as soon as you've emptied one side, the other calls your attention. And you're never quite certain which one it will be; all you know is that you can't leave the bathroom. I was suffering an intense bout of grief and betrayal poisoning.

The worst part of the betrayal was not that it took away the income Ric and I had been using to live—the income from the publishing rights to his music—and left me with two heavily mortgaged houses and tax bills I could not pay. I knew that I would figure out a way to survive financially. No, the worst part was that he publicly declared I had abandoned him.

After the funeral, time resumed passing, but in the oddest of ways. There were stretches where I felt like I had lapsed into a fugue state, finding myself at the store, or a friend's house, not knowing why I was there.

I tried to take my grief and shove it away. But it was just like pretending I didn't have food poisoning—it didn't work. Grief and betrayal consumed me, and there was no room to feel anything else. When I managed to pocket the devastation, I'd feel angry, and when I suppressed the anger, my sorrow climbed out of my pocket and threatened to smother me.

EVERY TIME I PASSED an art deco building with a sign that an apartment was available, I would start to pull out my phone so I could take a photo to show Ric later. I knew he wanted a prewar apartment because we had looked at places together when we put our house on the market.

I instinctively put his blueberry yogurt in my basket at the store every time I went grocery shopping.

When I saw a black-and-white sweater in a shop window while walking home from the supermarket, I thought, "Oh, Ric will like that," before remembering that I'd never again have the chance to give him a gift.

And throughout all of this, every single day, sometimes every single hour, came a barrage of emails from Mario, our business manager who was made the executor of the will that accused me of abandonment. Jeff had, at this point, suddenly made himself very scarce. The emails from Mario chased me for my signature, reassured me that he would be pleased to continue to be my business manager (and with a small discount too, because I had been such a longtime client), but to do that felt like I was submitting to the lie that I abandoned Ric.

And then there were the emails from well-meaning friends who thought I should see the dozens of tabloid articles popping up across the internet:

RIC OCASEK CUT ESTRANGED WIFE
PAULINA PORIZKOVA OUT OF HIS WILL

INSIDE THE "ABANDONMENT" THAT ROCKED RIC
OCASEK AND PAULINA PORIZKOVA'S MARRIAGE

WHAT REALLY HAPPENED BETWEEN PAULINA
PORIZKOVA AND RIC OCASEK?

The idea that I had to pretend I was normal, even though my life was imploding, was unbearable. I spent my days in lawyers' and accountants' offices, trying—and failing—to understand what they were saying. I could barely scrape together the concentration to have a casual conversation at that point, let alone follow the complicated legal and financial issues they were discussing. Thank God my girlfriends Anna and Jacquie accompanied me, asking questions, jotting down the information on their pads to later explain it to me, sometimes numerous times. My friends became my anchors, but even so, I could not escape the constant onslaught of demands requiring me to turn my attention to the betrayal every moment of every day.

THREE MONTHS AFTER my husband's death it was Christmas. There seemed to be an unspoken social agreement that I should be fine by this point. Once Christmas was over, it was a new year.

"New year, new you!"

"This is going to be a great year for you!"

"You have such a great new future ahead of you!"

"You have so much to live for!"

"You're free!"

"Look on the bright side!"

"You'll feel better if you put some makeup on."

My boyfriend, the man I had fallen in love with after Ric and I had decided to separate, asked me if I wanted to go with him to a meditation retreat. It was something he did every New Year. Neither one of us anticipated my reaction to his question. I fell apart. "And leave my grieving boys alone?" I exclaimed, and burst into tears.

"Oh, okay," he said, "I'll just go by myself then."

I couldn't—even if my life depended on it—explain how I felt. I knew I was supposed to be fine. But the pressure of trying to be "fine" made me feel like a stuffed doll, and his question had unzipped me, allowing all my dangerous, difficult, carefully contained feelings to explode out. He, very reluctantly, agreed not to leave. At the time, I was shattered by what I saw as his insensitivity, but in retrospect, he was in the very unusual position of comforting his grieving girlfriend over the death of her husband. He had no personal experience with grief and grieving, and my dithering made him impatient with what he started to see as my personal failings.

It was like when someone knocks on the door of the bathroom while you're still suffering food poisoning, asking when you'll be done.

RIC DIED in the middle of September. By October it had become clear that I would have to sue Mario and the trust that he and Jeff had set up, a trust comprised of all of Ric's assets. This meant I was to battle not only a man I thought of as one of our closest friends, but my own sons and stepsons as well, who were the beneficiaries of the trust.

Amid all this legal maneuvering were the questions eating away at me: How could I have been so naive? So stupid? How was I so wrong about the past thirty years of my life? So wrong about our love? So wrong about Ric?

A friend sent me an article about something called "complicated grief." Complicated grief is grief that refuses to resolve. It's often precipitated by an unexpected death and can be brought on by complications in the grieving process, like the loss of not only your loved one but also a loss of finances, or of your home, or of your standing in the world. But no one had really explored the complications of being betrayed by the same person you're grieving. I had no maps to guide me.

From articles on the internet, I learned that betrayal trauma, PTSD, and grief are related but separate diagnoses. Betrayal represents a traumatic death, not of a person but of a relationship, of trust. PTSD, post-traumatic stress disorder, can result in fear and problems caused by trying to avoid fear, while betrayal trauma can result in shame and dissociation. Grief,

of course, is an overwhelming sadness, which numbs and dis-
orients.

This information helped, but I could not find anyone who
had written or spoken about what happens when you discover
the betrayal at the same moment you are plunged into the
deepest, newest, freshest, most painful grief. I couldn't find
anything about what happens when grief, betrayal, and the
shock of finding your partner dead occur simultaneously.

And so, I was alone.

OVERTURNING THIS hastily written will, signed only a few
weeks before Ric died, was not the most important thing to
me. The most important thing was to make sure that Ric's
betrayal of me did not damage our sons' love for their father
or their trust in me. Because they adored him. They adore him
still. He was a wonderful father to them. I tried so hard not to
let my feelings of betrayal show. But I was still sick with my
bout of emotional poisoning. Just because I had gargled and
walked out of the bathroom didn't mean I felt fine. Not by any
means. In fact, the pressure to pretend I was okay made me
feel worse. There are moments I regret, moments when I raged
about Ric's actions in front of my sons.

But when friends would criticize what Ric had done, I de-
fended him. I still loved him. I love him even now. Only I was
allowed to say anything negative about him.

I was supposed to show the world how to overcome grief and betrayal—and money problems—with a smile. Set a good example. And I tried.

But I found that one of the side effects of grieving and suppressing anger—something that is rarely talked about and frankly is never accepted or even tolerated, but is inevitable—is a sort of self-focus that can be interpreted as selfishness. People get frustrated by your desire to stay in the bathroom. You know that you are still poisoned, liable to fall sick at any moment, but no one else seems to remember that. You can't get away from the pain. Your world has shrunk to contain only you.

A year later, when I managed to sell my house, my boyfriend declared he didn't have the fortitude to stay with me. He wanted a healthy relationship, and as I watched the movers dismantle my home of thirty years, he walked away without looking back.

IN WORLD WAR I, doctors introduced a new treatment for syphilis: malaria. Before the discovery of penicillin, doctors infected advanced syphilis patients with malaria to induce dangerously high fevers, fevers high enough to kill the syphilis bacteria. Of course, sometimes patients then died of malaria. But advanced syphilis—syphilis that had infected the brain—

was so terrible that the risk of dying from malaria was preferable to the all-out madness of neurosyphilis. It was called pyrotherapy.

One terrible, dangerous pathogen could wipe out another. The syphilis spirochete could not survive the heat of the fever. And sometimes the patient couldn't either. Doctors examined the pyrotherapy patient's blood every day, looking for evidence that the syphilis bacteria had been destroyed. Once they saw no more spirochetes, they quickly dosed the patient with quinine to try to cure him of the malaria and save his life.

Heartbreak, I learned, functions like malaria. It burned out the betrayal. The pain of the heartbreak caused by my boyfriend burned away the pain and anger caused by my husband's betrayal in some strange form of emotional pyrotherapy. I was finally left with only sorrow. The grief for my husband, the man I loved my whole life, remained.

My husband's betrayal, those few final words, now feels more like a crime of passion, an impulsive wound. I believe that what my husband did was unkind, but I now wonder if it actually came out of his obsessive love for me. The true end of love is indifference. And vindictiveness is not indifference. My husband may have been vindictive in his will, but I think it reflected a wounded and still-present love. Was his obsessive love healthy? Probably not. But I—a person who learned to enter the house of love through the chimney instead of the front door—can understand that he had found his own strange entrance. And I can finally just miss him with an uncomplicated longing.

Heartbreak is what cured me of the pain of betrayal. It is also what allowed me to become the woman I am today. A woman who understands she has made bad choices for good reasons. A woman who has learned lessons she wishes she hadn't had to learn, but is better for it. A woman who has discovered her worth by picking up the pieces of her broken heart, laboriously sewing it back together piece by piece, and, in the process, making it bigger.

It's not that what doesn't kill you makes you stronger. It's that what doesn't kill you makes your heart bigger—if you let it. In the process of mending your heart, you can make it better. You can cut out the assumptions and the judgment and stitch in generosity. You can rip out shame and sew in self-acceptance. Then you can stuff the whole lot with love and embroider it with gratitude.

HEARTBREAK

One velvety night in Buenos Aires, outside a café in a tiny cobblestone square, a woman with long hair swept by the rickety table where my friend Sheila and I were drinking wine. She fanned out a deck of tarot cards in front of us. Did we want ours read? Of course.

In a corner across the square, tango dancers performed their magic to mournful music played on old boom boxes. The women were beautiful and shiny in their tight dresses, the men dignified and in charge, spinning and pulling and dipping their partners. It looked effortless. It reminded me of the early years of my marriage.

"What do you want to know?" the woman asked.

After a very long marriage with a very long dissolution, I

wanted to know if a man would ever find me desirable again. She laid out her cards on the sticky table and frowned.

"Oh dear," she said. "The man in your future will break your heart. He will destroy you."

Bolstered by wine and the late hour, I laughed. "Well, then I will not fall in love with an asshole."

She looked at me sadly. "That's the problem. He's not an asshole. He's a good guy. But he will break your heart nevertheless."

Her prediction came to pass three years later.

HEARTBREAK IS A PAIN unacknowledged after a certain age. We've all suffered heartbreak as teens; we all got over it. As we get older, heartbreak is treated with less and less importance.

Grief carries dignity. Grief is respected, even when not shared or understood. Grief has gravitas.

Yet grief and heartbreak are both losses, both wounds to the heart. They both alienate you from everyone and everything. You're entirely alone and in pain. Managing either takes every ounce of our energy. Every menial task becomes a test of endurance. Yet while grief can be respected, heartbreak is dismissed.

I know this because I experienced both at the same time.

Our first date was in a museum. I suggested we walk through the museum, pick our favorite piece, and wait until the end of the date to reveal what we chose.

We both picked the same painting. A modest little watercolor of trees in muted tones. The two trees in the foreground of the painting bent toward each other, an invisible breeze allowing their branches to touch just for a moment so that the sun behind them created an exploding star right in the middle.

We met after my husband and I had finally shared the news of our separation with our children and the world at large. He was the first man in thirty-three years who had shown any interest in me. Sad and lonely as I was, I threw myself into him headfirst like you would dive into cool water on a hot day. I was too parched to examine what I was diving into. I fell in love, completely and passionately. For some time, he revived all the things that had once lived in me, things that had wilted so much I barely recognized their existence anymore.

The first time I followed him back to his apartment after a dinner date, I noticed a keyboard piano tucked away in a corner. While he showered, I pulled on my jeans and sweater and quietly padded over to it. I sat down, turned the volume on low, and played. A piece by Chopin.

I didn't hear him leave the shower and come up behind me, but as soon as I felt his presence, I stopped.

"No, keep going," he said. "It's beautiful." He sat in a chair nearby and closed his eyes to listen. I wasn't used to playing to an audience. I wasn't used to being listened to.

Even so, I could sense the rocks around me as I swam in the cool water, the warning signs, but I naively believed I should just swim out farther. The last time I had fallen in love, I was nineteen. I still believed love was an endless ocean.

For over two years I kept swimming and colliding into rocks. The man I had fallen madly in love with was generous, kind, a wonderful father to his children, and very funny. But our understanding of love was different. He often told me, "If we don't work out, I'll be sad but not destroyed." I chose not to believe him. Instead, I just thought I needed to keep swimming until I would reach a place where I'd no longer run into obstacles.

AND THEN, I had to sell the home I had worked my whole life to own, because I could no longer afford it. But that wasn't heartbreaking. No, the heartbreak came when this man I loved walked away from me the same day the movers were carrying all my possessions away. That day, as I crashed into an unforgiving barrier, I realized I had been swimming not in the boundless ocean but in a pond. In all fairness, he had warned

me. I should have known then that if you can't break someone's heart, maybe they don't have one to break. My boyfriend
never presented himself as anything but a pond. Clear, but
limited in size. I could have seen the boundaries, the edges,
had I wanted to look. But I was caught up in the feeling of
water after years of drought.

He left me standing in the middle of an empty house. There
was no furniture, no beds; I had sent the essentials to my boyfriend's apartment, believing we were to move in together. Instead, I ended up sleeping wrapped in a moving blanket on the
floor of my children's old room. I bought a bottle of whiskey
and a pack of cigarettes. I made a fire in the fireplace of my
now barren living room, huddled by it, drank, smoked—after
years of not smoking—and cried. The next day, I got into my
car, crying so hard as I drove away from the house and life I
had known that I could barely see the road.

My husband, whom I had loved and trusted for most of my
life, had been dead for a year. I still missed him every day.
And every day I was still angry with him. On top of my grief
about my husband's death and my anger at his betrayal, I felt
the sadness of losing my house, anxiety about my finances,
the shifting hormones of menopause, and now this, the final
blow to what remained of my heart.

Grief feels like drowning in a rough ocean, swamped by
towering waves crashing over your head, pulling you under.
It is part of nature, inevitable.

What distinguishes grief from heartbreak is that in grief, you fall overboard. The shock of hitting the water temporarily freezes you. You have no idea which way to go. You just tread water, trying to stay alive.

In heartbreak, you know who pushed you. You reach out your hand for help, and when they refuse, you try to pull them in with you. When that fails, you circle the ship, over and over, hoping to be pulled back aboard.

I READ EVERY BOOK on heartbreak I could find. All the books advised me to distract myself: Take dance classes. Travel. Go out with your friends. But none of these things were possible now that a pandemic had shut down the world. My friends and family had already borne a year of my grief, and they were also isolated and unhappy. Calling them to cry, again, seemed selfish. Everyone was suffering. People were dying. My heartbreak had all the importance of a summer cold. But that didn't make it hurt any less.

There were only two pieces of wisdom from all the books I read that I found helpful. One advised me to change my now-ex-boyfriend's name on my phone, so his name on any incoming texts would be less painful. He became "Mr. Emotionally Unavailable." I must admit that may have been my favorite advice. The second was from a Buddhist book that advised me to allow myself to give in to my pain and physically trace it. Where does it start? How does it feel? Observing the pain gave me respite from thinking about the cause of the pain. I noticed that the pain formed in my chest and radiated up my throat into the back of my mouth and my nose to spill over into my eyeballs. While the physical pain of grief feels like a tall, strong, cold person gripping you from behind, arms crossed over your chest and forcing your air out, the pain of heartbreak is more immediate. It is someone plunging their hand into your chest, taking a hold of your heart, and crushing it between their fingers.

The time following was the darkest and most painful of my life. The world was sunk in a worldwide pandemic. On paper, I was grappling with grief, betrayal, trauma, and heartbreak. In my lived reality, I was hurting so badly I wanted to stop being me. I continued to have Zoom sessions with my long-time therapist. But all I did was weep and spin in circles.

Of course, I thought of ending it all. Of course, I thought of taking pills and drugging myself into oblivion. Of course, I thought of going through the bottles of wine in the basement. What stopped me? It was the knowledge that I was standing on an edge. One small step meant oblivion. It was a way out of pain. But it would be final. Irreversible. I think it was at this point when all my memories and experiences gathered around me, holding hands, reminding me how much I had overcome already. My history of pain and love assembled itself and held me back. That, and my two sons, two young men whose umbilical cords, never mind how old, still tethered me to them.

IT TOOK ME over a year of circling the boat before I realized no one was ever going to pull me back aboard; no one was coming to save me. I had to swim back to shore on my own.

It was the longest year of my life. The tarot reader's words haunted me: "He will destroy you."

He had destroyed me. He destroyed the nineteen-year-old starry-eyed teenager who believed in love conquering all. He destroyed all the signposts I thought I had learned in life. The man I loved left me to drown to save himself. But instead of perishing, I found I could still breathe. He destroyed the girl I was and left something remarkable in her place. A woman. The old me drowned to make room for an amphibious creature, one who could move between water and air, pain and joy, with the understanding she was flexible enough to inhabit both. Perhaps a mermaid. The words of Anaïs Nin came to mind: "I must be a mermaid . . . I have no fear of depths and a great fear of shallow living."

In both grief and heartbreak, there is only one way forward. Once you start swimming in the right direction and you see the shore ahead, you know how to get there. When you emerge from the water, a new world is waiting to be discovered. You have learned that you can survive turbulent tides. You also understand the strength it takes. You know you can conquer anything, from a shallow pool to a stormy ocean. Your world has just grown larger, your empathy has expanded, and you're able to understand that sympathy and advice tossed at people swimming in the turbulent sea of pain are not life rafts. You'll know better than to tell a drowning person to be grateful for water.

REAL MONEY

It had to be close to one hundred degrees inside the van. Sweat gathered around my hairline and upper lip, my hands were clammy with it, and it ran down my legs in rivulets. This made putting on the damn woolen pantyhose especially challenging. Jessica and I kept bumping into each other as we tried to change clothes in the back seat of the van, which smelled of gasoline, powder, and onions. There was a rap at the window.

"We're going as fast as we can!" Jessica yelled out. It was the fifteenth outfit change of the day, and I knew the photographer was worried about the light changing. But when I looked up, it wasn't the photographer at the van window. It was three Italian teenagers, leering and laughing at our half nakedness. Jessica, who was an American model, looked horrified, and she quickly ducked behind the backrest, trying to wrangle herself into her knit dress. I ignored the boys and pulled my mohair sweater over my head, widening the neck with my hands as far as it would go so as not to smear my makeup. Still, the little filaments of mohair caught on my sweaty face and made me sneeze.

We were doing a catalog shoot in Rome, modeling heavy winter clothes in the middle of a piazza on a hot summer day with only a passenger van as a dressing room for five of us models. I just needed to get through the day and take a cold shower.

Catalog shoots were a model's bread and butter in the '80s. They were either hot, freezing, uncomfortable, or mind-numbingly boring, but they paid well. Every model, even the top models, did lots and lots of catalog shoots back then. You can go on eBay now and search for any famous model and a well-known catalog from back then and find some treasures. Catalog shoots paid well, and there were lots of them available.

Covers of magazines were prestigious but were also the lowest paying: a hundred dollars for a day of an editorial shoot, whether or not it included a cover. Ads paid better than catalogs, but the highest-paying ad campaigns called for well-known models, so you had to do the editorials to try to land advertising gigs.

I wasn't really, fully aware of the economics of modeling back then. I simply went on the jobs my agent booked for me. I didn't actually like modeling at all, but I liked being out of

Sweden, and I liked living on my own, and I liked having spending money.

I was a teenager in Paris suddenly making more each month than my mom and dad made in a year combined. School could wait. I had gotten lucky and needed to ride this as long as it lasted.

When I first arrived in Paris, my agency set me up in an apartment and paid my rent. My agency also paid for my plane tickets from Sweden to Paris, for all the test shots with various photographers, and for the hundreds of photo cards we used on go-and-sees. If you had acne, the agency paid for you to go to the dermatologist; if your teeth were bad, they paid for you to go to the dentist too.

They did not do this out of the goodness of their heart. They charged us for all of our expenses and took them out of our pay. In essence, the agency was lending each model money that would (hopefully) eventually be repaid when we were booked for jobs by clients. We were given little booklets of vouchers, and when we finished a job, we would fill them out and have the client sign the day rate and the hours worked. Then we submitted these vouchers to the agency. If you forgot to get the client to sign your booklet, you were out of luck and out of pay for the day. After the agency took their 20 percent commission, they charged us for all the expenditures they had shelled out for us, and only then would they tally up the sums and pay us at the end of the month. Many girls who went to Paris for the summer left at the end owing the agency large sums that could never be collected.

I was lucky. I was almost instantly in demand as a model. I made a lot of money, and quickly. I collected my money in cash at the end of each month and spent almost none of it. No one told me to open a bank account—I had no idea that I even should—so I just stuck the cash in a drawer until I went home for Christmas. Knowing it was illegal to transport large sums of money from country to country, I took a teddy bear someone had given me, ripped off his head, and stuffed my money into his body before sewing his head back on. I brought the bear with me to Sweden and gave my mom the money I had saved, so we could buy a house. By the time I was seventeen, there was enough to buy a small house on the outskirts of town.

It wasn't until I came to New York that money became something other than paper I stuffed into cheap toys. In New York, the agency had accountants who counseled me to get a business manager. I met a nice man in an office stuffed with memorabilia who kindly said he'd take me on as a client. His office would pay all my bills and give me pocket money. I had enough money now to rent a lovely apartment in downtown Manhattan, and I furnished it with a futon mattress. Then I made the biggest purchases of my life: a baby grand piano. And a Siamese kitten. That was all I needed.

When I met my husband at nineteen, I had been living on my own for four years but had always had someone else—

either an agency or a business manager—taking care of financial concerns for me. This suited me just fine. I had learned in Sweden, at the bottom of a toilet bowl, that money would not make me happy, so I didn't pay attention to it. Three years after Ric and I met, I left my own business manager and accountants and chose to use Ric's instead. He said his were better, and I didn't question him. We got a mortgage and bought a house in Gramercy together a year before we got married. But once we started talking about marriage, everyone—our business manager, my modeling agent, and Ric's music manager— all counseled us to sign prenups. My husband refused.

"It's a terrible way to set up a marriage," Ric said, "with the idea that it will not succeed. No prenups."

I wholeheartedly agreed. I would be married to this man forever. So what did we need a prenup for? That his first two marriages had ended in divorces did not even occur to me.

Thirty years later, we were embroiled in our own divorce proceedings. I thought it would be easy, or at least straightforward: we would split everything half and half. Right?

It turns out that when you hire very expensive divorce lawyers, nothing is easy. They will try to convince each party that the other one is cheating and wants too much. Each side will spend months demanding, refusing, and then finally poring over the documents. They will demand ridiculous concessions from the other side, who will in turn refuse and make their own ridiculous demands. This will go on for months, even years. Things get ugly and nasty. Whatever residual love and warmth there was between you disintegrates. In court, two or three years later, the judge will decide that everything should be split in half, but not before you've bought the very expensive lawyers a new tennis court.

In our case, it all became moot. Ric died early on in our divorce proceedings and left a will he had hastily signed a few weeks before major surgery, on the advice of his lawyers. In it, he decided to disinherit me, claiming I had "abandoned" him. For the next two years, I had to sue my own business manager, who was now the trustee of Ric's estate—and by extension my own children and stepchildren, who were the beneficiaries of the estate. It took two years for the estate to propose a settlement. During those two years, I learned more about money than I had in my entire life up to that point. My complete inattention to the money I had earned left me scrambling. The only cash I had between the two years after Ric's death and the settlement from his estate—the only money I had access to for living expenses—was from a cash-out mortgage on the house, which I was trying to sell.

When I fell in love with my husband, I was not yet twenty years old, still a teenager, and my accidental modeling career was beginning a precipitous climb to the top. I had never meant to be a model and didn't have much vested in my success, and so I merely showed up at the jobs my agent booked and then marveled at the benefits and rewards. I had no strategy, no goals, no plans on how to be as successful as possible as a model. It was just a job. It was easy to give it all up for something I considered to be a much more important part of life: love. That was something that had eluded me as a child, something that I believed was surely the most meaningful part of life.

I threw myself wholeheartedly into marriage. This meant a lot of caretaking, since my love was an artist and didn't like to do things like wake up early in the morning, or make any sort of arrangements, or run mundane errands like going to a store. I took care of him, his family, and, eventually, *our* family with the births of our children. Of course, having money made this a lot easier. We had an au pair and a housekeeper. But mothering and homemaking were the focus of my life, a focus I happily and freely chose.

When I accepted a modeling or acting assignment, I had to make sure it didn't conflict with Ric's work schedule—or his sensibilities. Some of the work I was offered was just too stupid or humiliating for me to do, Ric would decree. Such as: any movie with a love scene, and most modeling jobs. Initially, I objected. My pulchritude made me nearly the same amount of money as my husband's talent. But eventually I realized that my autonomy was the price I needed to pay for happiness in my marriage. I was willing to pay it. After all, love was more important than my career.

I still managed to make a lot of money. When I signed a contract with Estée Lauder in 1988, it was the largest modeling contract ever signed at that point. All that money went into the family purse. I had no real idea what happened to it— whether it was saved, spent, or invested. My money was rarely mentioned. It seemed to function only as *frivolous* money, something nice to have, while the money Ric earned was always the *serious* money, even when we made the same amount. Ric's money was the money that counted. He was the "breadwinner." Our business manager always spoke to my husband about our finances, and I would just get the condensed version from Ric later: don't worry. It was so nice not to have to worry.

But when my modeling career began to seriously fade in my midforties, it became increasingly clear to me that we had, in fact, for many years been living off my income as well— even if Ric and the business manager were not willing to admit it. In 2010, our business manager told us we were living above our means and would have to cut down on expenses.

The children and I flew economy, though Ric continued to always fly first class. I bought no new clothes for myself and started cooking every night, even if I was working during the day and my husband had spent the day playing video games. It was somehow understood that he played to restore and replenish that fantastic place from which he created, and so it was more important for him to relax than me, who just made pocket money with my trivial jobs.

When the dissolution of our marriage began, I was still good at being married. Or, at least, I was good at putting Ric's and the children's needs above my own. I knew that getting divorced would mean an even steeper adjustment in lifestyle, as it does for most everyone. But, somehow, the fact that I was no longer employable at fifty-three hadn't yet sunk in: my only education had been in how to look good in front of a camera while avoiding being harassed by horny men. Still, I thought, half of what we had accumulated after thirty years of marriage should be fine to live on, even if it wasn't in the "style to which I had become accustomed."

Instead of a super-friendly separation with mediators, as I had envisioned, my husband got a lawyer renowned for being ruthless. I had to get a corresponding shark. It seemed senseless to me to fight about money when the law was clear. We would both get pretty much the same amount whether we did it in a friendly, cheap way or a harrowing, expensive way.

We were still living together at this point. Still eating meals together, still going out with friends, still watching television in the kitchen before bed when the kids were home for breaks. We were still a family, even if we weren't living as husband and wife. I had a boyfriend, and he was meeting available women. But we were, I thought, friends.

After a few nasty exchanges with our lawyers, I swallowed my pride and once again begged him to reconsider the scorched-earth-style divorce. And he acquiesced. We decided to take it to mediators instead and remain civil. We could get apartments close to each other. Watch each other's pets. Celebrate family holidays together. Have weekly dinners. We hugged. He'd be there for me when I needed him, and I would be there for him. We put our house on the market while still living together.

Just a few months later, I was on vacation when he called and told me he had to have surgery. I told him I'd be there for him. I cut my trip short and returned home early. I got to do what I was good at: taking care of someone.

And then my husband died. In his will, signed weeks before the surgery—when I had come back to take care of him— he disowned me. Abandonment, it said. Suddenly, I was no longer entitled to half of our joint estate, but only a third. In divorce, one partner is not allowed to stow away or change their finances. But in death, you can make out your will to say literally anything. By law, death trumps divorce. Our business manager was made a trustee of my husband's estate, also perfectly legal, although I was now excluded, and so in effect, my own business manager was now to work against me, on my sons' behalf.

As my husband's widow, I inherited both of our houses and our pension plans. Our houses were both extensively mortgaged, and the pension plans could not be touched for another ten years. I had capital and no cash. I had to sell one of the houses immediately. But a worldwide pandemic had just started, and New York City was at the center of it. Everyone was moving out of New York, and property values had fallen off a cliff.

I found myself, at the age of fifty-four, after a wildly successful career and thirty years of marriage, with no job, no job prospects, massive tax bills looming, and no infusions of cash for another decade, when I could officially "retire."

I WILL NEVER REGRET prioritizing my children over my career.

But.

It turns out there is room for both.

I had an interesting conversation with a friend one evening in my kitchen over a bottle of wine. She was a new mother, and we were talking about parenting. She told me how much she loved her parents and what a great job they had done raising her and her siblings.

Knowing her dad had been a high-profile CEO of a large company and her mother a stay-at-home mom, I was curious about the division of actual parenting. I was shocked when she answered, "Oh, I'd say it was about equal." It seemed impossible. Yet she fully felt as if it had been equal. It was in that moment that my life and career choices flashed before my eyes. Could I have kept at my career without depriving my kids? I asked my boys if they felt like one of their parents had been more involved in raising them than the other. They responded with, "No, about equal." In a way I loved it, because I understood it meant my husband and I had made them feel this way: together, we had provided such a solid base that my children never felt deprived of either one of us. But on the other hand, *damn!* I wished I had made more space for my own career.

There is nothing wrong with wanting to be a full-time mother. It truly is one of the hardest, most fulfilling jobs. When my children were little, my modeling or acting jobs became my vacations. But it also dawned on me that being married and being a mom is a full-time job in which the rewards are only emotional. How many men would be willing to take a full-time job in which their only form of payment was sticky kisses and the acknowledgment one day in the far future that they did half the parenting?

I'm often asked what I would tell my younger self. What advice would I give to that girl struggling to pull on pantyhose in the back of a van, the girl who got paid in little paper vouchers turned in once a month for cash she stuffed into a teddy bear? The girl whose understanding of money never really developed beyond the magical notions of a teenager? In years past, my advice would have been, "Don't stress so much, everything will be okay."

Today, I have a different answer.

Yes, I wish I had signed a prenup, I wish I had kept my money separate, I wish I had kept working more, but most of all, I wish I hadn't handed over the purview of *me* to someone else. I trusted my husband. I trusted him to steer me in the right direction in every way to the point of self-abnegation: I gave up work, friends, and even my likes and dislikes for his love. And I learned the hard way that to nullify yourself means that when you most need yourself, you may not even know who you are. I had made choices, and now I was seeing the consequences.

It's taken three very painful years to learn lessons I would rather not have had to learn. But I have learned my worth. And I will never again settle for less.

SHOCK

I made another pot of coffee. Ric took his coffee with three-quarters of a teaspoon of sugar and just the right amount of milk to bring it to a very specific shade of beige. I poured the coffee into his favorite cup, the thin black mug with the white enamel inside, added milk and sugar, and walked up the two flights of stairs to the bedroom.

He had been waking up early since he got back home from surgery, but it was after 11:00 a.m. now. I thought it would be nice to bring him his coffee in bed.

It used to be our bed. We had shared this bedroom for twenty-eight years. But as often happens in middle age, Ric had started snoring all night and began sleeping in the guest room so we could both get a good night's rest. When he came home from the hospital, I cleared my things out of our bedroom and moved upstairs to the guest room, and Ric moved back into the bedroom. The bed was bigger and more comfortable, and there was an adjoining bathroom. It made sense. At this point, we'd been separated for two years and had been living in the same house like (I thought) best friends.

Our bedroom was large and high-ceilinged, our dark wood sleigh bed squarely in the middle. The drapes were already open when I entered the room. The sunlight was filtering in, catching a glint of gold on his finger, the art deco Egyptian ring he had taken to wearing after removing his wedding ring. He was still sleeping, as he always slept, on his back, one hand elegantly tucked under his chin, head slightly turned to the windows.

I put the coffee down on his bedside table, next to the box of tissues, his glasses, and an unframed Polaroid picture of our boys—at ages two and six—that had been propped up against the lamp for the past fifteen years. I turned to touch his shoulder, and it was then that I saw his eyes.

His eyes didn't look like his eyes anymore. I knew what those eyes should look like. I knew those eyes so well.

I touched his face. It was cold.

My legs went numb and collapsed under me. I sat on the floor, gasping for breath. Ric had just gotten back from major surgery, but it had gone well. He was recovering. He was on his way back to health. This just couldn't be.

I have no idea how long I sat on the ground. It could have been a minute. It could have been an hour.

It's like I had been swept off the deck of the cruise ship that was my life by an invisible wave. I was overwhelmed by icy black waters. Then, eventually, smaller waves of understanding crashed into me, orienting me in this ocean of the unknown: I have to tell our children. I have to walk downstairs. Move my legs. Stay afloat.

A list of what to do next unspooled in my brain. I thought to myself: "I will say, 'Guys, I have terrible news.' I will be calm. I will make it all right for them."

I commanded myself to get up and walk. I held on to the side of the bed to pull myself up. But when I tried to put any weight on my legs, I couldn't feel them. They were two limp noodles. I could not get on my feet.

It's an incredibly strange feeling when your legs give out. "My legs have given out," I thought. My brain was like a sort of split screen. There was a me who had ceased to function, and then another me who was narrating the events to myself, and still another me who wasn't functioning. "That's what that saying means. This is it. I'm weak in the knees. I've heard that saying. How strange. That's what this is."

Unable to get up, I crawled down three flights of stairs on my belly and elbows. There were sounds issuing from me that I was only dimly aware of. All I knew was that I had to get to my sons.

My older son, Jonathan, and his girlfriend were having their morning coffee at the kitchen table. The narrator in my split-screen brain was clear and firm: I could not let my son see me on the ground like this. "You have to stand up now," she said. I grabbed the railing on the last step, pushing myself into an upright position with all the strength in my arms and shoulders, holding on to the banister for dear life.

Jonathan saw me, his eyes widening.

"Your dad is dead."

The words just fell out, like a marble I had been holding in my mouth. For one brief terrible moment, time stood still as he looked at me. There was only that one look, and he screamed. He jumped from the table, running past me, still screaming. I crawled after him.

My younger son was upstairs, a floor above the bedroom. He came bounding down the stairs when he heard his brother scream. I didn't need to say a word. In some strange super-human effort, Oliver took one look at my face and leapt over me and an entire stair landing.

When I got back to the bedroom, I saw my sons at their father's side. Jonathan understood immediately and was scream-ing with raw unbridled pain.

Oliver was silent. He stood, leaning over his father. He touched his father's face, rubbed his hands. He peered into his open mouth and examined his eyes, like a scientist. He told me later he was trying to figure out how to reverse it, to undo the death. Somehow, in his mind, that was a possibility. He was trying to fix this.

MY HUSBAND PASSED in his sleep September 15. Ric had cancer and had just gotten home from surgery, but his death was entirely unexpected. He had been recuperating well; his cancer was stage 0. This was not supposed to have happened. He was only seventy-five.

People gathered at our house all week. Food appeared, I don't know how. Time stopped existing in its normal state. There was morning and night, and the hours between stood still, winding forward and backward arbitrarily. The day before the funeral my friend Tracy gently told me it was time to take a shower, wash my hair, and brush my teeth. I don't think I had done those things for a week, but I can't remember.

The world around me ceased to exist as I knew it. Or, rather, everything stayed the same, but I could no longer relate to it. A desk was no longer a desk; it was just an object I had to navigate around. I'd find myself at the stove holding a pot and a spoon, not knowing how I got there, why I was there, or what the pot and the spoon were for. All the things around me became shapes without meaning, an obstacle course.

My memories from this time are completely unreliable. How many times did we make the drive from Gramercy to Dutchess County? Who drove? What did we eat? Who was there? Some memories stick out like shards of glass, so sharp they can still pierce the skin: the last song Ric wrote for me on replay in my headphones, Jonathan being held by his friends as he sobbed, a bowl of trail mix on the kitchen table, picking clothes for my husband's casket, his shoes lined up in the closet, his shoes! But my other memories from this time are as indistinguishable as a sea of mud. This intense fog, this feeling of inhabiting a different reality, persisted for three months.

PULL YOURSELF UP by your bootstraps. Impossible though it was, I attempted it. I had to be strong for my boys, who had descended into the same hell. If it weren't for my children, my only wish would have been to be left alone to rock and moo. This was the only thing I was actually good at during this period of time.

I'd sit down, and these strange sounds, like a loud hum, would somehow emerge from me. I realize now that these were the same sorts of sounds I made in childbirth. An anguished kind of a moan, almost like a cow mooing. These sounds were the embodiment of this pain that was inside me that needed to come out, and it took the form of these long, vibrating tones. I would cross my arms and tuck my chin to my chest. I would try to make myself smaller, curling into a ball, protecting my body. I rocked and mooed. I was trying to hold myself together. I had this urge to contain all I was. If I had let my arms drop and straightened out, I felt like my soul could vanish, evaporate entirely out of my body.

The pain of childbirth and grief reduces you to being an animal. One is physical pain, the other emotional pain. That sort of pain takes away all ability to reason. You exist suspended in time and agony. Nothing else matters. Only the pain is real.

I FELT LIKE I was going crazy. Cut off from everything and everyone in an alternate universe in which I was the sole inhabitant. Desperate for a hand or a light to guide me through, I turned to my lifelong source of comfort: books. But I'd pick up a book only to find myself unable to read. The letters jumped around and rearranged themselves, forming sentences that made no sense. Sometimes, I would hold up a page and think, "Ah, it's written in Swedish, that's why I can't understand." Only it wasn't. It didn't matter what kind of book I picked up—English, Czech, Swedish—the words rearranged themselves into ones I didn't know. Eventually, though, my reading ability came back, and I found all I wanted to read was someone else's experience of grief. I needed to see my feelings reflected in other people. I needed the hand, the light, that would help me navigate. But most of the books either told me to be grateful—that grief was love with nowhere to go—or told me to sit with my pain and let it flow through me. But at that point, the words seemed so trivial, so small, they couldn't possibly cut through my fog and pain. If anything, they pissed me off. I had turned to books precisely so I wouldn't have to be alone. I wanted company. Other people who understood what I was going through. Instead, I got platitudes. Well-intentioned for sure, but all I could think when I repeatedly encountered them was: "The road to hell is paved with good intentions." I needed a warm light to make me feel less lonely in the darkness, and instead I got lots of descriptions of what a light looked like.

I'm sharing my story to be a light for you. It's not a big light. I can't save you, and I can't make this better for you. But I am holding a candle, to let you know you're not alone, and you will make it through this.

If you are there now in the dark rocking and mooing, know I'm your company.

COURAGE

I readied myself for the forty-five-minute subway ride from Manhattan out to Brooklyn. I was fifty-three, and I was about to pose for a nude photo shoot for *Sports Illustrated*. At home, to prepare for the expedition, I filled my spray bottle with water and packed my paper fan—an old-fashioned item that I snap out and wave with a rhythmic cadence of my wrist—for when I needed to wet my face and get air moving over it. I checked that my bottle of antianxiety medication was in my bag, just in case. Just knowing it's there helps me, even though it takes an hour to kick in if I take it. I dressed in layers, ready to shed down to a cotton tank if needed, even in the middle of winter. All the layers have to be easy to remove, cardigans or zip-ups. Nothing over the head. I packed tissues, a doggy bag in case I (or anybody else on the subway) threw up, and a Zip-loc bag full of ice.

I thought of all possible scenarios. The train stopping, the lights going out, the conductor announcing something omi-nous over the PA system. This being New York City, the PA system on the train is always totally unintelligible, and I would have no idea what the driver just said. It could be that we were stopped temporarily, or it could be that we were all going to die. We could be stuck in the car in the middle of summer—the doors won't open and the air conditioner goes out and we're trapped for hours, trying to claw open the windows as we slowly cook. In winter, the rails on the Manhattan Bridge could freeze over and the train could skid off the tracks and career into the river. I've taken classes on what to do if a ter-rorist sets off a bomb or throws an explosive in the train (don't try to run—get down on the ground), as well as classes on what to do if someone attacks you with a knife or gun. I'm prepared for anything.

Finally, I headed out the door and started walking to the nearest subway station.

This is my routine—my preparation—every time I leave the house to go on the subway.

Contrast this with the preparation I needed to take the nude photos once I got to the photographer's studio: I took my clothes off.

I'm often told that I'm a brave person for modeling nude,

for standing in front of a photographer with no clothes, for daring to show the world my apparently shocking over-fifty-year-old body. I realize that for some people that would take a lot of courage. But that is not what takes courage for me; that is not where I need to muster all my strength and be brave. For me, bravery is leaving the house.

I HAVE SUFFERED from an anxiety disorder for most of my life—ever since I was taken away from Babi, my grandmother who raised me, and the world I knew. I had my first panic attack at the age of ten, in the middle of the night at my father's house. I was sleeping in a little rollaway cot at the foot of his bed, my four-year-old brother in a separate cot next to me. I woke up feeling sure that I was about to die. My heart was slamming so hard against my chest I thought I could see it pulsating through my rib cage. The air had suddenly become too thick for me to breathe. It was like trying to suck in oxygen through a straw. My whole body shook. My father and his new girlfriend were sleeping in their big bed. I barely knew them. I had lived in Sweden a year at this point, but I longed for my grandmother. She was back in Czechoslovakia, unable to leave while I was unable to return. My father and his girlfriend were two strangers to me; I wasn't sure that they liked me or wanted me to be there. Waking them up to tell them I was dying was a scarier prospect than just carrying on with death.

I rolled out of the cot and crawled to the bathroom. The toilet was in its own little room with a bright yellow light overhead. It felt like there was a huge, jagged rock inside me that expanded with every breath, squishing aside my lungs and heart and other organs with every gasp. The cold tile floor hurt my knees. My heart kept punching my ribs so hard it was as though it were trying to escape. I sat on the floor, rested my head on the toilet seat, and waited to die.

COURAGE IS OFTEN INVISIBLE. So we may not even recognize it in one another.

No one gives me a standing ovation for getting on a crowded bus. And no one applauds you for jumping into the pool, or speaking in public, or climbing a ladder to clean the gutters, or whatever else may terrify you. What I think is brave may be an everyday occurrence for you, and vice versa. Our courage lies in facing our fears, whatever they may be. Our fears, and how we build the courage to overcome them, are as varied and individual as our fingerprints. Our battles may seem small to someone else, but this in no way diminishes the courage needed to fight them and the strength we build up when we do so.

Clearly, I survived my first panic attack. But they kept happening. My mom was studying to be a nurse, so I used her medical textbooks to diagnose myself with a heart arrhythmia.

But I didn't dare mention this diagnosis to anyone, especially not my parents, who already seemed to find me undesirable. If they found out about my heart condition, they might abandon me again. It was like I was walking on a very narrow ledge, and any gust of wind would take me down—on one side was sudden cardiac arrest, on the other, abandonment. So, I'd clean the bathtub, change the litter box, do the dishes, make the beds, feeling like Cinderella while waiting for my inevitable death. Instead of a ball, I'd go to heaven, and surely my mother would be sorry then. Especially when I wasn't around to do the housework.

I WAS DIAGNOSED WITH ANXIETY in my early twenties. I was delighted to know that I didn't have a heart arrhythmia and that I was not going to die. Well, at least not from a heart arrhythmia. But it turns out there are a million and one other ways to die. People with anxiety tend to fall into two categories: the ones who fear they are going crazy, and people who fear they will die. I'm the latter.

Anxiety is not easily defeated. Once I lost the fear that my heart was going to take me down, I began to obsessively think about all the other possibilities. Plane crashes. House fires. A burglary gone wrong. Scaffolding collapsing on me as I walked underneath it on the sidewalk. Tsunamis. A giant icicle spearing me through the top of my head. Being stuck in the middle of the ocean on a boat that had run out of gas in a storm. What I began to notice was that the situations I most feared were all ones where I wasn't in control. Where I was at the mercy of nature, of chance, of other people's bad decisions. It's the same sense of helplessness that I feel every time I walk into a packed elevator, get stuck in a traffic jam, or see the doors of a crowded subway car slide shut.

I've been told that posing naked at an age when you should be invisible is brave. American women are taught that removing your clothing is like removing your protective suit of armor. Revealing your flaws is incomprehensible in a culture that thrives on imagined perfection.

European culture differs in this way. Nudity is more acceptable, at any age and any size. Revealing your flaws is the equivalent of an open hand: Look, no weapons. Nudity was common in Sweden, where I grew up. It meant being absolutely free and unencumbered. This is how I still feel about it today. Being nude, I feel free.

My true vulnerability lives in the things no one can ever see. The symptoms of severe anxiety are internal.

I have had all kinds of therapy, but ultimately, I have accepted that I am a person with anxiety, just as I am a person with blue eyes, a person who likes to read. I've learned to cope with my anxiety attacks through breathing techniques. And carrying ice. And the spray bottle. And all the rest. I've created a safety system for myself. This coping system does not eliminate the panic attacks, but it does mitigate them. It arms me for the battle. It allows me to live in the world and do the things I want to do, even though I know it will hurt, even though I know it will be a struggle every single time.

Learning not to panic when I can't breathe. Learning to stay when I want to run. Learning to look when I want to avert my eyes. This constant war with myself has, in fact, made me who I am: brave enough to leave the safety of a marriage, brave enough to rebuild myself and my life, and brave enough to talk about it.

No one is born with courage. It is built over the course of a lifetime. It's not just the moments that have made your heart break, or race, or bleed that have made you brave. It's your response to those moments. It's your willingness to confront your pain and fear. I built my courage one subway ride at a time. You build your courage your own way, by confronting your pain and fear, whether or not anyone else can see or understand them.

Being courageous hurts. It's a painful process. But if you can accept this—if you can overcome your reluctance to engage in something difficult and scary—you will come out braver than you were yesterday. You can be the hero of your own life.

NUDE, NOT NAKED

Strips and swathes of feathery black lace mingled with the shine of black leather. I was choosing what to wear from this rack of clothing, an unusual proposition when one is a model. Models wear what the client wants them to wear. We are there to make a garment look good, not the other way around. But that day all those little bits of black fabric were there to make me look good, to make me look the way I wanted to look.

I chose a few pieces, all lingerie, and began to try them on in the small, cozy bedroom with warm red walls and an antique bed. Luigi, one of the two photographers, came in to help me decide. Fishnet stockings, long soft leather gloves, thigh-high boots, lacy panties.

In the living room—a Victorian parlor beautifully arranged

with antiques and heavy curtains—a huge roll of gray paper was suspended from two poles in the middle of the floor and pulled down to create the ubiquitous background that serves as a backdrop to many photo shoots. Two umbrella lights and a camera on a tripod were also already set up. We were shooting in this home for a photography book that Luigi and Iango were working on, creating beautiful photos of beautiful women.

"We want to capture you, you at your most magnificent. The most you," Iango told me. "You as a woman, not a girl."

Standing on the paper, surrounded by flashes popping, I suddenly realized the netting and ribbons and fabric I was wearing were distracting. I was modeling the clothing, just as I had for forty years. But now, at fifty-six, with the majority of my professional career behind me, Iango and Luigi wanted to photograph just me.

So, I took everything off. In my nudity, I felt the most me. I liked myself. I liked my body. I felt free.

I was enough. My body was enough.

Stripping away the unnecessary lingerie was my way of reminding myself that the best version of me was the one without any ornamentation, the one with nothing to hide. My body was not offensive, it was not wrong, it did not need to be hidden or obscured with lace and netting. The lingerie did not make me more beautiful, because my body was beautiful enough. My body was not broken because of its age.

This was not a new revelation or an epiphany. It felt more like the period at the end of a sentence, a culmination of what I have learned.

GROWING UP IN SCANDINAVIA, there was no stigma around nudity. It was common to see nude bodies in magazines and on TV, and to see topless women at beaches, pools, and parks. On a few occasions, I even saw women driving topless in the summer. To be nude was normal, liberating. I developed an easy connection to my nude body. So when asked to pose nude in Paris, I would strip down without the slightest hint of shame.

In 1985, I was booked for a bathing suit shoot with *GQ*. The photographer was someone I enjoyed working with, and I was to pose for some photos alongside a male model who'd be unveiling the season's hottest bathing suits for men.

We flew to the Caribbean island of Saint Thomas for two days of shooting. Because the story was on men's bathing suits, I was supposed to be the background. The bikinis I wore were of little consequence, so I didn't blink at removing my bikini top and, for one photo, my bikini bottom, to suit the photographer's vision.

I was not known as a bathing suit model until I appeared in the *Sports Illustrated* swimsuit issue in 1983 and got the cover in 1984. Before then, in Paris, I was rarely asked to wear swim-suits because I didn't have the rounded hips that the swimwear industry preferred to see in their models. I didn't disagree, judging myself to look more like a test tube than an hourglass.

But in the time between my *Sports Illustrated* cover and the *GQ* men's bathing suit shoot, things had changed drastically for me. Quite literally overnight my name became attached to my image. Before that, I was the model with long brown hair and blue eyes, or the model on the cover of last month's *Mademoiselle*. Now, I was Paulina. Or, more accurately, Paulina Po— What's her name?

I appeared on late-night talk shows, did interviews, and was suddenly tasting a little bit of fame. I received piles of fan mail from young men and offers of dates from famous rock stars and actors. But while I was now sometimes recognized on the street as I walked to work, I was still just one of the girls when I got to a job.

One day in April, I was at the agency dropping off the pre-vious week's vouchers.

"Did you see the new *GQ*?" my booker asked.

"Ah, not yet." I was not terribly interested or excited. I knew she meant the shoot with me presumably in the back-ground, behind the male model posing in his new Speedos for the season.

She pushed the magazine across her white desk in the crowded room where all the bookers sat. On the cover was a photo of the architect Helmut Jahn in a fedora. And then there, in bright yellow, the words:

PAULINA AT THE BEACH:

THE ETIQUETTE OF TOPLESS

The headline didn't even make sense. It literally meant nothing. I still believe to this day that they really wanted to print WE HAVE PAULINA TOPLESS INSIDE!!! but it sounded too crass, and they tried to class it up.

This was not the deal I agreed to.

Posing topless or even fully nude didn't bother me at all. But using my being topless as a major selling point felt dirty. Suddenly I went from being carefreely nude on a sunny beach to being sold as an object of sexual desire. I had never felt ashamed of my nude body before. But now I did. I felt ashamed, powerless, and used. I had gone into the job as the background girl to sell men's swimwear, and without my knowledge or consent, I was now teaching the world the "etiquette of topless."

I was in Japan once for a shoot. It was late and I was watching TV, exhausted but jet-lagged and unable to fall asleep. Across the screen, a commercial appeared, featuring photos of Cindy Crawford and myself, advertising an escort service. Suddenly I was wide awake.

That *GQ* cover felt very much the same way.

Nudity itself is not shameful. But being sold as an object of sex without your permission is what makes you feel vulgar and cheap.

AFTER THE *GQ* SHOOT, Ric put his foot down. Our relationship was still a secret at this point, but he didn't want me to do any more nudes. He wanted me all to himself. He seemed to feel that my nudity was only for him. I had to battle with myself over this, because I felt my body belonged to me. He got to touch it; that was my gift to him. I believed that it was my decision how I chose to use my body. But I gave in. Peace in our relationship was ultimately more important to me.

Today, I still sorely regret not doing a nude pregnancy shoot with Irving Penn, one of the greatest fashion photographers of all time, when asked. And I still regret that Annie Leibovitz shoot where she wanted to drape me in wet white cloth, but I insisted on being more covered for my husband's sake. I called him in the middle of the shoot to let him know they were going to coat my torso in rubber instead. Curiously, the rubber made me more self-conscious. It made me feel as though I was trying to hide something shameful, a dirty secret, which had not existed until I decided to hide it.

After Ric and I separated, I happily jumped on the chance to be photographed nude for *Sports Illustrated* again. They wanted to do a series of nudes in black and white, with words that were important to us written on our bodies. I chose to have only one word, "truth," stenciled across my chest. Although the studio was freezing on a February morning, and everyone around me was wearing winter jackets and hats, I was happily and freely nude in front of the white background. I was liberating myself from being someone else's possession. I was fully inhabiting and celebrating the fifty-two-year-old body that had gotten me this far.

When I met the man who became my first boyfriend after Ric, the man I'd fall in love with, I made sure he knew how I felt about my body. He could borrow it. But it was mine to do with as I pleased. He was supportive—until I did a nude shoot for *Grazia* magazine and showed him photos of the session. "I guess I'm gonna have to be okay with knowing everyone can see my girlfriend's nude body," he sighed.

I just shrugged. Yup. I was never again going to let anyone else dictate what I could or could not do with myself.

When a commenter on Instagram claims I should be ashamed of posing nude because I should instead be making cookies and rocking my grandchildren on my knees, or when *GQ* puts a headline on a cover claiming I'm teaching the etiquette of being topless, or when my lover wants to keep me all to himself, they are all doing the same thing. They may not see it; they may think they are on opposite ends of the ethical spectrum. But it's really all the same thing. All of them are trying to take away my power—my choice—to exhibit myself as I see fit.

BEING NUDE is not the same thing as being naked. Being nude has purpose. It is a choice—it's choosing how you want to be seen. You're nude when you're posing for art.

Being naked is being vulnerable. You're naked when you're born, when you're in a doctor's office, when you're made to go through the X-ray scanners at the airport that undress you on monitors. It's certainly not a self-chosen celebration of your body.

Nude and naked are not the same, and they are both entirely separate from pornography. What turns nudity into pornography is not the reveal of a body, but rather the expected titillation. It's when attention is drawn to body parts with the sly implication—the hint, the wink, the nudge—that they should not be seen. It's the suggestion that seeing these body parts is scandalous or illicit. Shouting "See Paulina topless!" is what turns a nude into pornography. Paradoxically, drawing attention to nudity by strategically covering it often does the same thing, as it did when the *New York Times* took a beautiful nude photo that Sally Mann took of her innocent and free five-year-old daughter, and put X's on her nipples and between her legs. Suddenly, the photo now screamed, "Look! Inappropriate!" It's the covering of the nudity that made it inappropriate.

The first time in my life that I was exposed to pornography, I was around eleven years old, seeing a Georgia O'Keeffe exhibition at the museum with my dad. Standing next to my father, I marveled at the colors and shapes, until a man slunk beside me, pointing to the very painting I was admiring, raised his eyebrows, and snickered, "Vagina." His tone was leering and inappropriate. I initially had no idea why the man said what he said—it felt totally out of context—but in the tone of his voice was the insinuation that I was looking at something forbidden or lurid. It made me ashamed, though I didn't know why. Suddenly, the painting transformed. The lush pinks and the undulating curves morphed right before my eyes into a shape I recognized from sex-ed classes. It was like one of those optical illusions, where at first you see a fancy white goblet, and then suddenly, somehow, see two profiles facing each other.

Once the man moved away, my reaction changed again. Now, I was ashamed that I had been ashamed. There was nothing wrong with vaginas. Vaginas were normal and could be the source of a lot of good feelings: this I learned in school. Yet I knew I was blushing. I didn't want my father to see me react with shame to something that I knew wasn't shameful. I flushed with confusion. I quickly walked away, pretending some other painting at the opposite side of the room had caught my interest.

IN THE WORLD OF ART, a nude male often signifies power, whereas a nude female often signifies sexuality.

I did an internet search for "older woman nude in art," "elderly woman nudes," "old woman paintings nude," and half a dozen variations of the theme. The results were a few Lucian Freud paintings of full-figured women (most of whom were not actually elderly at all); paintings by a female artist named Aleah Chapin, who began a series of nude paintings of proud naked older women in 2011; and some "granny porn" sites. That was the extent of the representation of the bodies of mature, sexy women.

If women are valuable to men only as sexual creatures, as fecund and fertile, then that will be the only way we are portrayed in art. This may be why a nude of an older woman, no longer in her childbearing years, draws such criticism. She is seen as trying to incite desire for a body that can no longer reproduce.

A nude of a naive, virginal teenager is more socially and artistically acceptable than a nude of a sexually mature grandmother, who clearly got to be a grandmother exactly because she is sexually experienced.

I'M PROUD OF MY BODY, this body that has borne and fed two children, that feels pain and pleasure, that takes careful dedication to maintain, that has brought me here, at this precise moment of being fifty-seven, and finally, finally fits me. My skin may no longer be taut and plump, but its softness and drapes contain all that makes it work. My muscles may no longer be as strong, but my delicate skin makes them more obvious. My bones may ache on rainy days, but they are holding me up with more assurance.

In Luigi and Iango's living room, I stand on the gray paper, a fan blowing wind through my hair and caressing my skin. The lights pop. The Bee Gees sing about staying alive. I raise my arms up to my hair, the wind, the music, the lights celebrating me. "Beautiful, magnificent, stay there, hold that, gorgeous!" the photographers call out.

Nude. Nothing to hide behind.

I have nothing to hide.

MEDICATED

S o, I just started . . ." I began, then hesitated. Was this the right place to out myself? At this table with five beautiful women, none of whom I knew all that well besides my friend Liz, who had brought me here? I felt like I was carrying this big, shameful secret, and the weight was just begging to be unloaded. We sat in a private room of a fancy restaurant. We had all already spilled a glass or two of white wine, and tongues were loosening, mine included.

"Started what?" Kerry, dressed in head-to-toe cashmere, prompted me as she refilled my glass.

I decided to proceed.

"I've had this crushing anxiety, ever since I was a child, and last year, after I got booted off *Dancing with the Stars* and started promoting my book, it just got out of control."

The ladies were attentive. One was a lawyer, one was a journalist, one a photographer, and two were formerly high-powered executives.

"So, I started on an antidepressant," I finally blurted out. I felt shame wash over me.

Liz, who sat beside me, laughed. "I've been on them for twenty years now," she said casually. "Best thing I've ever done."

And then, to my utter amazement, the rest of the women followed suit. There were six of us in one room, middle-aged, with careers and kids and marriages, and all of us were medicated.

I started taking Lexapro after my anxiety attacks came back and, for all intents and purposes, crippled my ability to function. I've always had anxiety attacks—or panic attacks, as some know them—but after years of learning how to deal with them, I thought I had them under control. While my kids were little, the anxiety attacks even subsided to the point where they hardly bothered me. But as I turned forty, they came back worse than ever.

I couldn't get in a car, a bus, or even an elevator without panic overwhelming me. I'd find myself unable to draw a proper breath, my heart would pound, and heat would flash through my body, making me break out in sweat. To top it off, my PMS—frustration, depression, and irritability—started stretching two to three weeks instead of the typical one.

I've never liked the feeling of being reliant on medication of any kind (please, I had two kids unmedicated, I could take some pain!). But my doctor suggested that I deserved a break from anxiety. Rebooting the system, he called it. He also fully supported the idea that I begin talk therapy, but in the meantime, he offered me the following analogy: You can build a house with your hands, or you could use power tools. Either way, you're building a house, right?

I had just gotten kicked off of *Dancing with the Stars* (as the first contestant of the season to be kicked off), and my ego had regressed to ninth grade, when I was the least popular kid in school and just couldn't figure out what I had done wrong to be so disliked. But I had to get over myself, quick. I had children who needed me. I had a husband who needed me. I also had my novel (which had taken me five years to write) to finally promote. This was no time to sink under!

Lexapro it was.

At first, the medication didn't seem to work. It wasn't until a few months into treatment that I realized what had happened. My inner world had quieted. The constant hum of anxiety became noticeable only by its absence. It was like spending your entire life in a room buzzing with the sound of fluorescent light, and then, one day, you suddenly notice the sound has stopped. I wasn't quite sure what to do with this silence, how to live in it.

Shortly after starting to take Lexapro, I was booked to be on the panel of judges for *America's Next Top Model* (*ANTM*).

I had to have a physical for insurance purposes, and so I truthfully wrote down the only medication I was taking, Lexapro. Unfortunately, this was promptly broadcast all over the *ANTM* production set. Apparently, I couldn't be properly insured on a TV set if I was taking an antidepressant. I had just started taking it, and this reaction was exactly what I had feared. I was judged crazy. Unstable. It was almost enough to get me to stop taking it before it had even had a chance to work. Fortunately, the woman in charge of all this paperwork laughed and admitted that she was also taking said medication—weren't we all? The production could just sign a waiver, taking their chances with crazy ol' me. And they did.

As I became braver, as I dared to speak more openly about what I perceived as a terrible weakness, my friends, one by one, stepped up and admitted that they were also on antidepressants. One friend took it because she was depressed. Another took it because she got too angry. Yet another also suffered from anxiety attacks. The reasons were diverse, but what we had in common was that we were all women, all of a similar age, and all married with children.

This shocked me. It also got me wondering. What was going on here? Was this a sort of universal malaise that hit perimenopausal women who were married with children? Was this the female equivalent of a stereotypical male midlife crisis— Botox and antidepressants instead of the fast car and affair with a younger woman?

I SPENT TWO YEARS with Lexapro, the most mellow two years of my life. My immediate frustrations were comforted, my resentments muffled, my anxiety calmed; I was wrapped in a thick, warm comforter, insulated against the rough blows that came with living.

But I was also insulated from fun things, like my creativity and my sexuality. I used to joke to my friends that after twenty-four years with my husband, we were, sexually speaking, a finely tuned precision engine. But now it felt as though I was being touched through a thick and cumbersome rug. After a while, it seemed like being intimate was just too much work for too little pay.

And as for creativity, well, with my new sense of peace, I found I had no need to actually express anything. This, for a writer, is akin to a cook who has no appetite. Sure, it's possible to work, but the results will be uninspired at best. I no longer bothered to fight with my friends or my husband; I could just shrug and walk away from situations. And so, for two years, I learned nothing new. I felt emotionally Botoxed. Who was I under the blanket of medication? What did I really feel like? I began to wonder and to want all my feeling back, even at the steep price of misery.

Weaning myself off Lexapro was predictably unpleasant—three weeks of being tired and shaky from wrangling with awful dreams. And then anxiety came creeping back: the clamminess, the suddenly speeding heart, the flashes of heat, the disorientation. But this time, I also became aware of something I may have previously neglected under the loud hum of anxiety, or failed to identify, or perhaps simply didn't have before: depression. It could have been circumstantial: after all, with my career at a crossroads, my children no longer needing me every minute, and my face and body beginning to cave under the demands of gravity, I had reason to be a little down.

With the medication, I didn't feel like me, but without it, I also didn't feel like me. At least not the me I remembered, the one I wanted to be. My kids got to know a whole other side of their mom: an irrational, frustrated, weepy woman who had previously appeared only when I was alone. Now she was everywhere. I felt sorry for myself, and then terribly guilty, because I felt I had absolutely no right to feel sorry for myself. The world seemed to be too heavy to carry by myself, but I could not ask for help, because I didn't know how to ask. Nevertheless, there were moments of sunshine. And I could feel its warmth and take pleasure in it rather than just noticing it. It was a sharper joy. I had highs and lows, as opposed to just middles, and I preferred that existence. But I also discovered that exercise, of any kind really, helped to balance me out. I started to take kickboxing and dance classes between the days of Pilates and aerial yoga. Unlike the medication's side effects, the side effects of exercise were nothing but positive.

The years since have been filled with a fair amount of misery and soul-searching—but also learning. I am on a sort of accelerated life comprehension program I didn't sign up for but nevertheless must work through. This has gotten me thinking: Could it be possible that some of these difficult feelings are growing pains? Perhaps they are necessary to cross to the other side, where peace and confidence will finally triumph. After all, it's not just teenagers who have to adjust to changing hormones, and most of us can still remember the misery of those adolescent years.

I'm starting to wonder whether antidepressants can often be the emotional equivalent of plastic surgery for middle-aged women. With them, we can stave off the anguish of change; we can take breaks from the afflictions of living. But is it also possible that through their use, we pay another price: the price of going through life somewhat anesthetized?

I will never cease to be grateful to live in a time where knowledge has made it possible for people to no longer suffer. But would that knowledge exist without a little suffering? I'm certainly not an anti-medicine crusader—modern medicine saves lives. There is a large percentage of people for whom an antidepressant means the difference between life and death, or, at the very least, the difference between a life worth living and a life to be endured.

After my husband's death and the complete unraveling of my life as I knew it, I elected to face it without medication. But the mere knowledge that the medication was out there, available if I was in too much pain, gave me the courage to process the pain. I was struggling—and am, to a certain extent, still struggling even today—but the pain feels formative, important. But if the moment arrives where I feel like I've done the work, yet my life has not improved, I would not hesitate to give myself a medicated break. You know the saying "What doesn't break you makes you stronger"? What that saying skips over is the fact that before we become stronger, we need to heal. But in order to heal we need time. We don't hesitate to take a pain reliever when we are in acute pain, and medication that relieves emotional pain can be just as useful to take the edge off so we can find our inner resources to keep going. And sometimes, when we have done all the work but are still left with darkness, isn't it wonderful to know there is a little pill that can make it bearable?

OCCUPIED

I was busy rehearsing my poem for a first-grade competition. It was about the Russian people, our "best friends and saviors," who had liberated us Czechs in our time of need. Babi sighed, just home from work, setting a little bundle of red paper rectangles on the kitchen table where I sat memorizing my poem. Babi always sighed a lot when she was unhappy, a sure way to let the household know her displeasure. If no one asked her what was wrong, she'd begin to mutter to herself under her breath. And if no one took her up on that, she'd go on to roll her eyes and eventually escalate to making Anna Karenina—esque threats of throwing herself under the train.

Babi started her muttering. Uh-oh. I caught some words, bad words, like "go to hell," "damn," and, most egregiously, "stupid Russians." We had been told at school that if we ever heard anyone say something bad about our "friends," we needed to report it to our teachers. Would I have to report Babi? I jumped off the chair so I could pretend I hadn't heard anything. "Babi, what's that?" I asked, pointing to the stack of red papers she had put down, hoping to distract her.

"Flags. For the windows." She rolled her eyes.

"Oh, let me, let me!" I begged. I was relieved—Babi was only angry because she had to paste the flags onto her perfectly cleaned windows. I grabbed the little stack. Each rectangle was a print of the Soviet flag, bold and red with the gold emblem of a hammer and a sickle. I would paste them on the windows. It would make me a good citizen, and Babi would stop frowning.

I picked up a roll of tape from the kitchen drawer and went to our living room, which we used only when we had guests. The two large windows were facing the street, the best place to put up the flags. Painstakingly, I set them just so, in the right-hand corner of each window where everyone else had theirs. Up and down our street, little red rectangles appeared in every household window. Any window not decorated meant that a bad, capitalist-scum family lived inside. Our bedroom also faced the street, so I pasted flags in those windows as well. When I finished, I still had two flags left, so I went to the family room to paste them on the windows there, even though those windows faced our garden and no one but us would see them. Proud, I ran out on the street to admire my handiwork. The flags in every spotless window looked like happy red hearts, I thought.

SINCE BEGINNING GRADE SCHOOL, I'd had two fervent wishes. The first wish, the most important one, was to see Lenin embalmed in his glass casket in Moscow. This was a pilgrimage everyone aspired to. Lenin was part father, part favorite uncle, and part Mikulas (the Czech version of Santa Claus). In photos, he was gently holding children on his lap, or lambs in his arms, or petting dogs. He wasn't just tender, he was also strong. He could be seen standing sternly in front of a waving Soviet flag, an arm raised, ready to battle the evils of the world on our behalf.

My second wish was to become a Pioneer. A Pioneer was a child who'd achieved perfection in doing good deeds and being a good Communist. Everyone admired their little red neckerchiefs. You could not become a Pioneer until fourth grade, but I was already on the lookout for good deeds.

When we were six, my cousin Hana and I once tried to help an old woman cross the road. With a nod to each other, Hana and I both moved to opposite sides of the woman, grabbed her gently but firmly by the elbows, and half-pushed, half-walked her to the other side of the road. Once there, she looked at each of us uncomprehendingly.

"Why, girls, did you make me cross the street?"

Hana and I traded frowns of incomprehension.

"I was just trying to remember where I put my keys," the old lady wailed. "Walking hurts my old bones, and now I have to cross that damn street again."

Proving we didn't yet have it in us to be good Pioneers, Hana and I simply ran away, mortified, instead of helping her back.

But carefully pasting the Soviet flag in the corner of every pane of glass was just the sort of thing a good Pioneer would do. I was proud to do my duty.

WHEN MY MOTHER SUDDENLY reappeared in my life after years of absence, I accepted her and my new younger brother without question. But what was harder to accept was the influx of information she shared that was diametrically opposed to everything I knew and everything that had made me feel safe.

Now, I was privy to outbursts from my mother that technically would prevent me from achieving my two great wishes: to become a Pioneer and to visit Lenin. This beautiful woman, who was apparently my mother, was frequently speaking ill of our best friends. She went much further than my babi, who would throw warning glances at her, saying, "Anichko, careful. Language." I knew I ought to report my mother to my school authorities, but I also knew I never would.

Czechoslovakia was, at one time or another, part of the

Austro-Hungarian empire, Prussia, Germany, and, lastly, the Soviet Union. Centuries of occupation turned us into a people who threw up our hands in the face of aggression. Instead of fighting, Czechs went and got a beer. The most militant protested by throwing themselves out windows. Our country was abundant with beer and castles and was centrally situated within Europe, and the only resistance any invader would face would be a couple of self-defenestrating dissenters. Honestly, why *not* invade us? It's a wonder that we managed to hold on to any shred of national identity and language.

My mother was an oddity. She was fearless, oppositional, and a troublemaker. She married another troublemaker, my father. When the Soviets invaded Czechoslovakia in 1968, she and my father saw a life of menial jobs ahead and decided to risk their young beautiful lives to escape that fate on a motorcycle. When she came back to Czechoslovakia three years later armed with a fake passport, a wig, and glasses to try to reclaim me, she was arrested. She was held in a jail cell and interrogated by police while seven months pregnant. Nevertheless, she stuck by her fake name and her fake story. I'm sure she would have never caved. What ultimately gave her away was when the police placed her in a lineup and asked her friends and family if they recognized her. Almost everyone denied recognizing her. But one foolish—or perhaps terrified—friend exclaimed: "Anna! So good to see you back!"

After that, she was under house arrest at her parents' home.

The Czech police took an apartment directly opposite our house, so they could keep tabs on not only my mother but also anybody who came by to visit. Anyone who visited would then encounter harassment and intimidation at work. That my mother still managed to maintain friendships under these conditions was a testimony to her incredible charm and social skills.

Despite being closely observed by the Czech police, my mother remained fearless. She loved listening to Radio Free Europe. It was the only place you could hear information about the outside world. You could listen to music that wasn't Russian approved; you could learn that there were other choices out there, choices that weren't available to us here. Listening to Radio Free Europe was also dangerous and very, very forbidden.

I knew I would never turn my mother in, but I feared someone else would. This became an everyday fear for me, an undercurrent running below everything I felt. There were also moments when I was angry at my mother for some trivial thing or another, and the idea that I could report her made me feel powerful. It made all of us children simultaneously very powerful and utterly powerless.

When, three years after their arrival, my mother, my brother, and I were released to go to Sweden, I was afraid. Sure, I was excited to see my dad, or, rather, to meet him again after six years of being fatherless. But what I knew of capitalist countries didn't seem alluring. It didn't matter how many times my mom would describe how nice Sweden was, that you could have a banana or an orange anytime you wanted, that there was more than one Barbie doll in the window of the local toy store. No. In my mind, anywhere not under the protection of our best friends was a wasteland of blackened trees where people could pop out from piles of garbage and casually shoot you while you walked down the street.

It wasn't until we reached Sweden and I could see it all for myself that I understood that what I had been taught my whole life was a lie. Sweden was beautiful and peaceful and immaculately clean. No one owned guns. I finally got my long-coveted Barbie doll. Bananas were so abundant that they would sit turning brown on our countertop. My mother and father and all their friends could say anything they wanted. I wasn't required to report anyone for anything.

I never reported my babi or mother. But I reported other kids. Anna didn't post a flag; Lena rolled her eyes when we sang the Soviet anthem; Martina left her Pioneer scarf outside in the rain. I alleviated my guilt and shame over not reporting my family by reporting other, less important people in my life. Nothing happened to those kids. But, of course, reporting children wasn't the point. The point was that we were being taught that it was natural and good to turn in your friends, so that once we reached adulthood, you would have no qualms about turning in your colleagues at work, your best friend, your lover.

We were indoctrinated to believe that anyone in our lives—our classmates, our friends, our partners, even our parents—were disposable. That our true parents were the state. Our true family was the Communist Party. The party would take care of you and all your needs. They would never abandon you. Your loved ones were not reliable in the way the Communist Party was. Your family had no power. You could report them whenever you got mad at them. This undercurrent of distrust is the most damaging part of living in a totalitarian country. No one is safe. All relationships are suspect.

This is the true horror of occupation. It's not what you can see, it's what you can't. It's not the lack of shelter, the long food lines, the censorship, the lack of material choices in one's life. It's the lack of privacy of thought. You are not allowed to think. For if you think oppositional thoughts, you may accidentally reveal them when you're frustrated or when you confide in a friend. And if you do, you may lose your life as you know it. Your mind—your thoughts—has been invaded.

It is *you* who has been occupied.

If you can trust no one, how can you love? And how can you be loved, when your thoughts are not your own?

You're squashed into a container that may fit you when you're a child, but once you start growing, you must be crushed and rearranged so you continue to fit within the tiny container destined for you. After years of being crushed and rearranged, even if you're eventually released from the container, you've lost the ability to stand.

Perhaps this is one of the contributing reasons why I was so happy to be molded and owned by the man I loved.

My marriage was a sort of occupation. At nineteen, I watched Ric roll into my life in his tank, and I greeted him with flowers and cheers. Being occupied made me feel safe. I was home.

With age and maturity, I slowly began to outgrow the boundaries imposed on me. So, it was with shock that I eventually realized this occupation of me is what I still, today, construe as love. It's what I still desire. It's what makes me feel loved, an outside force that sweeps me up off the ground and deposits me into the world of the one I love: "I want you all to myself, all the time, I want you to spend every waking moment with me, I need you to complete me." This is my damn chimney into the house of love.

MY RUSSIAN POEM won that first-grade competition. I can only remember the last line: "The Soviet Union, our best friends!" My reward was a Russian fountain pen. It never worked.

I HAVE, by now, learned that being owned is not the same as being loved. And that occupation doesn't mean I don't need to fear abandonment. Quite the contrary. When the occupier abandons their territory, what they leave behind are people who never learned how to stand on their own. What happens to your relationships when there is no freedom of thought? If you can't think for yourself, who are you? You are an assemblage of someone else's thoughts and desires. You are valuable only to the one who assembled you, and only as long as you function as specified by their rules.

Or at least I hope I have learned this. I'm not sure. The truth is that it frightens me that the words I still long to hear are "You belong to me."

I can only wish I've learned enough at my age to understand that a tank rolling into my life is not a liberator or a savior or a protector. That the safety I long for doesn't come armed. What I hope for are not two countries merged into one—rather, two countries with open borders. What I hope for is that I'm no longer undefended territory waiting to be occupied.

EVERY WOMAN IS
BEAUTIFUL

I woke up and opened my eyes. Well, sort of. I squinted them open. Even without looking in a mirror, I knew they had swelled up overnight. A quick visit to the bathroom mirror confirmed the transformation. Two giant-size strawberries had replaced where my eyes had been, complete with little seed dots, and my actual eyeball—a blue marble—barely visible in the center.

It didn't particularly alarm me. I had, after all, paid money to look like this.

I knew that in about three or so days the swelling would go down, and I would be left with dozens of purple polka dots around my eyes, scabs that would eventually peel off a few days later. I gently patted on the serum my dermatologist had given me. It burned a little, like a sunburn.

The doorbell rang. Of course. On the way to the front door, I grabbed my enormous Jackie O–style sunglasses and put them on so I wouldn't startle whoever was out there. What the UPS deliveryman thought of my look—pajamas printed with cat heads, accessorized with giant sunglasses—at 7:30 a.m., I'll never know, but I was pretty sure I had just averted a possible 911 call. Yes, I looked that scary.

I had gone to a dermatologist's office to have these little dots burned into my skin. All this in the quest of boosting a little natural collagen. Which would, presumably, lift and tone the areas around my eyes. How much? Probably not a lot.

Why did I put myself through this? Because I'm a woman of middle age. I have been rendered invisible by our society's standards of beauty. My whole life has been based on visibility; it has been my bread and butter since I was fifteen, and the loss of that is also the loss of a large part of my identity, the me I knew. I'm now the woman who buys every new cream on the market that promises to smooth and lift my skin, to erase my wrinkles. Even though I know better, even though I know there is no such magical potion in existence that can actually turn back the clock. Turn back to what? Youth, which is where visibility resides.

IRONICALLY, in my youth, when most women are considered to be at the height of their beauty, I blabbered on and on about looking forward to aging. To me at the time, aging represented wisdom and confidence, both of which I sorely lacked. I was aware that I was valued only for the way I looked, not for all the other parts of me, and I imagined with age I'd gain the wisdom and confidence I longed for.

The French have a saying that has always stuck with me: Age is the revenge of the ugly ones. How I loved to quote it when I was a young woman. I had, after all, been considered ugly as a teenager in Sweden, and so even when I was on magazine covers, I still did not see myself as pretty or beautiful. So I thought I understood the saying. I had no self-awareness of how pathetic it must have sounded to everyone around me: this young girl, considered beautiful, making an enormous amount of money off her looks, spouting "truths" about things she knew nothing about. I was a pretty young thing, but I longed to be a woman of character. What did that mean to me, to be a woman of character?

I wanted to be a jolie laide.

ONE LATE EVENING in Paris, after exiting a nightclub, my friend Jacques and I sat eating French fries and drinking White Russians in the Publicis Drugstore. It was a sort of small mall selling all sorts of odd and ends: electronics, medications, cigarettes, ice cream, and burgers late at night. We sat by the windows that faced the end of the avenue of Champs-Élysées, looking out at the spotlit Arc de Triomphe and wolfing down fries.

And then she walked in.

Her hair was a messy dark bob, her lips a dark red slash below a protruding hooked nose. Her eyes were dark and close-set, her skin pallid. She wore jeans, a white-and-blue striped boatneck, with a bulky motorcycle jacket thrown over her shoulders. Her unabashedly sticking-out ears were accessorized with large gold earrings.

She was unquestionably ugly, I thought. And she had, rather perplexingly, taken care to highlight every one of her flaws. But she flung herself down on a chair at a nearby table with the confidence of a queen. She ordered an Irish coffee, lit a cigarette, and, within a few minutes, had captivated a whole table of guys, who started to clamor to buy her a drink.

I didn't get it. Was she famous? I asked Jacques.

"I don't think so," he said, after ogling her for a bit. "But she is *vachement* cool, don't you think?" He pronounced the word "cool" in a short and percussive way, making it sound French.

I stared at her. Cool? Yeah. I guess. I watched her laugh, putting her high-heel-clad feet on a nearby empty chair. Okay, no, she *was* cool. Very cool.

"She is a what we call jolie laide," Jacques said. Between bites of soggy fries, he went on to explain how "jolie laide" translates to, quite literally, pretty-ugly. It seemed the French kept a certain celebrated spot on their beauty charts for women like this one, the unconventionally attractive.

"If you have a girlfriend like that"—Jacques nodded her way—"you are cool too. You know?"

I hadn't known, but as I watched this woman, her beauty started to come into focus. She was ugly, but in a sort of delicious way. The more you watched her, the more beautiful she became. That slash of red across her lips that originally made them seem thin was sensual; instead of plump and cushiony, hers were like a narrow opening into secret pleasures, private ones you'd only discover if you got past the acerbic wit they uttered. Her pronounced nose with its bump in the middle looked regal. Important. The sticking-out ears were rather perfect to tuck away her messy curls.

By the time we paid and got up to leave, I knew I needed to immediately buy a red lipstick, a blue-and-white striped boatneck shirt, and a leather jacket.

"THE UGLY MAY BE BEAUTIFUL, the pretty never," wrote Tom Robbins in *Even Cowgirls Get the Blues*. There is a difference between prettiness and beauty. Anyone can appreciate prettiness. It's easy to look upon, in part because it's a little bland. Like a pop song that you like right away, at first listen.

But it doesn't stick. It's not memorable. It's not unique. In fact, it's the opposite of unique: if it pleases a multitude, it has a sort of middle-of-the-road characteristic that will offend no one, and, therefore, thrill no one either. Prettiness is simple: it is youth and symmetry. A symmetrical face with no marks of aging will, almost always, be seen as pretty. It is fresh, it is alive, it is shiny. It is attractive. But is it beautiful? No.

A jolie laide is unique. Her looks might offend you. But you won't forget her. Her beauty lies exactly in the fact that she is not easy to take in at first glance. Unlike smooth prettiness, a jolie laide's beauty is sharp. It wounds you a little and leaves a scar.

Beauty, unlike prettiness, is not dependent on smooth reflective skin or symmetrical features. It doesn't rely on conforming with what the culture around you has deemed worthy of attention. It can be ugly, if you consider ugly the opposite of pretty. It's not that beauty doesn't coexist with youth, it can. But it's not youth dependent. Real beauty is often secret, like that of a jolie laide, only discoverable with a little patience.

Invisibility is not from a lack of beauty. Invisibility is from a lack of attractiveness, a lack of prettiness. Older women often become invisible because they're no longer considered attractive. We're invisible because we no longer attract attention from other people. This is part of the challenge of dating in middle age, but it isn't only contained to romance. We don't attract the attention of the waiter. We don't attract the attention of the salesperson in the shoe store. We don't attract the attention of the butcher at the supermarket when we're trying to order a turkey for Christmas dinner. We don't attract the attention of our boss at work, no matter how good our reports are. We're invisible because we don't attract attention. We are not attractive. We might be—in fact, I'd argue, we *are*—beautiful. But beauty and visibility are not in fact necessarily linked. If you are beautiful but not pretty or attractive, you may remain invisible to most. Only the connoisseurs of beauty, a select bunch, will notice you.

A symmetrical young woman is pretty. By that definition, the marks of aging are not pretty. Marionette lines around the mouth, hooded eyes, and crow's-feet are not generally considered pretty.

I'm not making the tired point that everyone is beautiful on the inside. Rather, I'm making the point that everyone *is* beautiful on the outside. We have been trained to overlook beauty in favor of prettiness, freshness, youth. But as prettiness fades and what we think of as the ugliness of age emerges, it actually allows us to see the character, the physical beauty in faces. In every face.

Regardless of what I think of my own aging face and body, I look at you, a woman of a certain age, and I think you're beautiful.

I love the hooded eyelids. They are sensual and a little sleepy. A little bedroomy. Like you've just made love and fallen asleep and the pleasures of your body, the rumpled sheets, have imprinted themselves on your eyes.

I love the 11s between your eyebrows. They make you look like a woman of deep thought. A woman who hasn't let her life go by unnoticed.

Your crow's-feet? They are maps of laughter. They are your history of squinting at the sun, of smiling at those you love, of the most joyous moments of your past.

I love the lines around your lips. Maybe you were smoking cigarettes late at night in a smoky club, or maybe you have kissed so many people in life that the kisses have etched their way onto your lips forever.

The lines across your forehead are a reminder of every bit of excitement and delight you've ever witnessed, the presents you've opened, the open arms you've fallen into, all your moments of the unexpected and new.

The tendons in your neck look like the sails that cut and navigate the winds of your life. They lead you forward. Your neck looks strong, powerful. It shows the courage and the power of holding your head up, holding up the history of your life.

The crepey soft skin that gathers on your belly and on your legs and arms, why not think of it as the rumpled silk sheets on a bed in the morning? It's far more interesting than a smoothly made bed. It has a history of making love.

I love the life you've lived, etched in your face and body.

The history of your life written in your skin. That's why you are beautiful.

WHY CAN'T I FEEL the same way about my own face? Why do I need to go and have little dots burned into the skin around my eyes with lasers that heat up and wound my skin so that it needs to rebuild itself a tiny bit smoother, a tiny bit thicker? Why can't I resist every new age-defying product on the market? Why do I have to battle my face in the mirror every day?

If only I could feel the same way about myself as I feel about you.

Perhaps it's a matter of comparison, not between you and me, but between me and myself. Me as a young pretty woman and me as an older woman of character. A face with character is a face that is an original work of art. A face of beauty.

I have to choose between battling two wars. Either the war against invisibility or the war for self-acceptance.

In the war against invisibility, I can battle my own face with the help of professionals. I can erase lines and sags with modern technology. I can buy myself some more time at the main table, where the action of life happens. I can use Botox and fillers and scalpels to be pretty again, but at the cost of losing the characteristics that are unique to me, and which I've worked so hard to achieve. Tweaking with Botox erases wrinkles and, with it, character. Botox erases beauty in favor of prettiness. I understand why so many women get Botox and fillers. Those procedures help us regain prettiness—they buy back some visibility in the world in a way that our beauty and character will not. For those of us who want to be visible, it may seem like the best option. But which do I want more: Visibility or character? Prettiness? Or my life, with all its joy and grief, written on my face?

In the war for self-acceptance, I have to battle myself, not to erase but to acquire: confidence, self-assurance, and acceptance. I want to be seen for all that I am: the good, the bad, the beautiful.

FATE AND CHOICE

Pani Rusova was a short woman of indeterminate age, pleasantly plump, with a helmet of curls that had been permed, sprayed, and dyed strawberry red. Other women her age wore drab skirt-and-sweater sets over their expanding middles. But Pani Rusova dressed in bright pastels and accessorized with scarves and jewelry, looking completely incongruous in our little town of Prostějov. She was a parakeet among sparrows. She lived in our house, in a tiny room upstairs with no plumbing, so she had to come downstairs to our apartment to use the toilet or get water. As a child, I never questioned her existence in our lives. Only after I became an adult did I begin to wonder about her life story. But all I managed to find out was that she may have been Jewish and had hidden during the war.

When we lived in the house together, I'd go to visit her in her little room upstairs. Her door was often open, her single bed with its lace bedspread by the door, and a desk by the window, where she kept a water jug and a bowl for washing. The rest of the tiny room was occupied by knickknacks, which I very much admired. I especially admired the bouquet made from stalks of oats, each little oat painstakingly wrapped in the shiny colored foil paper you got from hard-candy wrappers. It was not each stalk that was wrapped in paper, but rather each tiny individual oat in the stalk, each smaller than a pea, nestled and overlapping one another. It would have had to take weeks to create a whole bouquet of them. So much of our life in Czechoslovakia looked drab, gray, and beige. The buildings were covered in soot and our clothes all washed so many times they had lost their color. But this. This was pure color. Pani Rusova had created something magical from just candy wrappers and oats. I was mesmerized.

"Pavlinka," she would say, "come here. I will show you something funny." Czech was her second language, so she never quite got the grammar right. She couldn't pronounce the Czech soft *r*, admittedly one of the hardest sounds in all languages to get right. She didn't actually mean "funny," she meant "fun." And she *would* always show me something fun. A new bottle of peach-colored nail polish, with which she would paint my pinky—only my pinky, because nail polish was expensive, and she didn't have much money. Sometimes it would be a new lipstick—she'd let me sniff the powdery sweet scent when she twisted it open. Once, she showed me how to make those beautiful shimmering oats, like the ones she kept in a vase. We sat down on her bed and she pulled out a drawer, revealing all the colored foil candy wrappers she had collected. I watched as she cut a piece of candy wrapper into tiny squares with her manicure scissors and then, painstakingly, wrapped each little oat seed. I thought it was the most beautiful thing I had ever seen in my life, festive and glittering, reminiscent of Christmas, the only time of the year when our gray world turned sparkly and magical with lights and colors.

The palm reading was an afterthought, something she did once at the end of one of my visits. She picked up my hands and traced the lines on my palm, explaining what each one meant.

"See, this is line of love, up here," she said, pointing to the first line below my fingers. "This is line of head, how you think like, yes?" she continued. "And this, line of life, how long you live." She traced the long, rounded line that arced down toward my wrist. "The little breaks in line, it is changes. Maybe good, maybe bad." She wasn't any more specific than that. But I became intrigued, and, afterward, would pick up my friends' hands and with great authority predict their futures.

It was fun—a party trick. It became especially popular in Paris, and especially with men. No one objected to my picking up their hand to read it.

I kept at it until I met a young man at a dinner gathering. Olivier looked like a soccer player—brown curls, a roguish smile—and he sat next to me at a long table that was covered with sheets of paper on top of the tablecloth, a French custom in the more informal cafés or brasseries. We drank red wine, ate steak au poivre with frites, and flirted. He told me his family owned vineyards and that he would take me to see them. Perhaps the following weekend? After he had completed some car race he was to participate in. I picked up his hand.

"Let me see if I'm here," I said, "in your love line."

He put both hands on the table, palms up. "And if you're not, I don't get a date?" he joked.

The first thing I saw was that the lines in both of his hands were the same. I had never encountered that before. And his life line on both was very short.

"Well," I said with a laugh, "according to your hands, you ought to be dead already."

"So, if I am alive next weekend, tell me where to pick you up."

He took my number. We shared a sweet kiss outside the café before I hopped into a cab. I waved at him through the taxi window.

We never got our date. He died in the car race.

After that, I was much more careful about reading palms. Given enough drinks, I'd pull my trick out again. But I knew now not to reveal anything bad, to speak only of things that could have a positive outcome. I did so many palm readings that I developed a sort of instinct. I got very good at it. While sitting in the recording studio as my husband produced the first album for a new band called Weezer, eight months pregnant and knitting baby sweaters, I read all the hands I was given. The bass player, Matt, ended up memorializing that moment in a song called "Friends of P."—the first single he released as a member of the Rentals, a band he formed after leaving Weezer.

Today, when I meet someone new whom I like, I try to read their hands as soon as they'll let me. For me, it's like getting a very brief instruction manual, written in a language I'm only passably good at deciphering—a glimpse into the essence of that person. I often see more than I tell, but much of what I see is a feeling, an illuminating sort of a flash that comes and goes.

Your two hands differ from each other. The left hand is the hand of fate. It reveals the things destined for you. The right hand is the hand of change. It reveals how your current mindset affects your actions and can therefore alter your fate. Only very rarely do both hands agree exactly, as in the hands of Olivier.

Much of what I see can be shrugged off as coincidence. No, I'm not always right. And yes, I can read my own. I have always known my life would change drastically around fifty. I assumed it would be an illness, and then I would keep going. I have two major loves in my life, my love for Ric clearly marked and long, bisecting my emotional health and my line of luck, which generally means that it affects those areas of your life, for good or for bad. My second great love I hope and pray hasn't happened yet.

When I met the man who became my first boyfriend after Ric, I read his palms and was dismayed I could not locate our love on his palm. Where was it? I decided palm reading was bullshit but kept rechecking his right hand, just in case anything changed. The last time I checked his hand, our relationship was long done. He had made it very clear he only wanted to be a friend yet still, I wanted desperately to find myself in his hand. He flinched when I sat down next to him and turned his palm up. His was the same as ever. Lots of slight, unimportant lines crowding the heart line. I showed him mine.

"See, here you are." I pointed to the deep line in the middle of my heart line. He exhaled, with frustration it seemed, closed his hand, and moved away from me. It was devastating to understand that in his life, I was just one of many, when he had been so important in mine.

So maybe the hands didn't lie after all.

I HAVE A HARD TIME trusting my gut because I deal with so much anxiety, but hands are real. Solid. In front of me. The lines are right there. Your hands are *you*. Unique to you.

But some interpretation is necessary.

I look at the events in someone's hand and I read them, my way. This is what it comes down to. My view. My interpretation of the moment.

How do you choose to interpret a life? How do you choose to make meaning of the good and the bad?

When I was a child and my parents left me behind, I believed they had done so because of my large ears. My father owned a motorcycle, and when he was in the right mood, he'd let me sit in the front, on the gas tank, while he slowly cruised up and down the street. "Go faster, Daddy," I begged, and he would just laugh. "I can't go faster, because with your big ears, you'll catch too much wind and sail right off" he joked. When they disappeared from my life, I knew it was because they had wanted to go fast.

That's how I made sense of this, the only way I could understand why they could have left me. That was how I interpreted my life as a young child. It's not how I would interpret the events of my childhood today. This is the rather wonderful thing about aging. The longer you get to live and experience, the better you can interpret. And the better you interpret, the better choices you will make.

As I mentioned earlier, each of us has two hands. The left is the hand of fate and the right is the hand of choice, and they are almost always different. I look at it like this: Fate puts you into a world where you are at its mercy. You are born into circumstances that are beyond your control. Things will happen—fortunes and misfortunes—to you and to those you love. But. You have the choice to interpret them how you want. This is the only thing within your control.

You get to choose what your life means. You get to choose how to make meaning of what fate has given you.

Accepting the job of interpreting the events in our lives is where our power and, ultimately, our peace come from. You can interpret your way to your purpose. If you don't try to make sense of all the events that befall you, you become a dandelion seed in the wind, continuously carried about with no sense of direction.

Do I believe in palm readings? Yes and no. I believe what I want to believe. I'm not religious, but I have faith that there is something larger than myself. The idea of fate comforts me, because it allows me to believe that my life is guided by some greater meaning or purpose.

We all imagine we want nothing more than to make our own decisions, because then we'll be able to have control over the uncontrollable. But when I make the wrong choice, I find myself wishing I had known better. If I put my hand into an open flame, it won't do me much good to wish there had been no fire. My being placed next to the fire is fate. But what I choose to do with the flames is my choice. It's my decision to put my hand into the fire or to put the fire out. Fate, if it exists, is only a framework. Our continuous choices are what make us who we are.

I WAS GIVEN a book on palm reading, a sort of how-to manual. Much to my surprise, when I began to flip through it, I realized that the way I had been reading palms was different from the "official" accepted method. My method of interpretation had little to no overlap with the method outlined in the book, nor with subsequent books and websites I explored. I was shocked, truly baffled. "Well, they got that wrong," I thought, reading page after page. I thought about all the times I had been correct in my readings, all the people who had come back to me weeks or months or years later and said, "You were right!" How could I have been right so often while doing something completely different from the norm?

Well, part of it, I think, has to do with confirmation bias. We're much more likely to remember the times we're right. Not many people would bring up a reading years later to remind me of all the ways I was wrong.

But I also think that palm reading is not a science. There are fate and choice in your palms, yes, but there is a third ingredient in that mix: interpretation. That's where the real magic lies. How to interpret your own life, or someone else's.

Pani Rusova had shown me the basic lines, but then left it up to me to interpret what I saw and felt. She left it up to me.

———

I LOVED VISITING Pani Rusova. I could spend hours with her in her tiny, color-filled room. But when she would venture out into the backyard in her two-piece, flower-print, orange bathing suit to lie among the flower beds and get some sun, I felt ashamed. Out in public I was ashamed of her bright colors and eccentricity, even as I loved it at home. I somehow knew, even as a child, that a middle-aged woman was not supposed to be so bright, so bold, so visible.

Standing out in a Communist country is not, generally, a good thing. And if Pani Rusova was indeed a Russian Jew who had survived and escaped Russia, even more so. Standing out was a courageous choice. A choice she made despite what fate had handed her. A declaration of her uniqueness. She would not be invisible.

I still have no idea who Pani Rusova actually was—her background, her life story. But what she taught me, in addition to palm reading, was that you can create beauty out of anything. My interpretation of beauty may be different from yours; you may find all these shimmering bouquets of oats kitschy or tacky. But one's beauty should never be hidden, regardless of how others perceive it.

It is, after all, just a matter of interpretation.

ACKNOWLEDGMENTS

Writing is a solitary task. And, usually, a long process.

When I was offered to write a book in three months, it was a challenge I wasn't sure I was capable of. My novel had taken five years to write. I had just returned from shooting a reality TV show in the jungle and was physically exhausted.

My book agent of seventeen years, Marly Rusoff, is a woman of enormous knowledge, experience, and intuition, and when she recommended, given the very tight deadline, that I hire someone to help me and keep me on track, I didn't hesitate. Besides, I needed to learn how to write an essay, since I just signed up to write a whole book of them.

She introduced me to Kerry Egan, without whom this book would never have existed. Kerry, a phenomenal essay writer whose book *On Living* I devoured in one sitting between tears and laughter, became my rock. She was my reader and critic and teacher, and very quickly became a dear and trusted friend and confidante.

Acknowledgments

Each day, over Zoom and our morning coffee, we'd chat, and she'd give me a very clear-eyed review of the material I had sent her the night before. We disposed of politeness very quickly in the process and jumped right into "This beginning is really boring; you need to set the scene better; this essay is actually three separate ones; this ending doesn't work; and this essay has no point."

She was merciless and brilliant. But quick to compliment when I came up with something good. I couldn't have done this without her. And while we are at it, if you hated the book, it's all her fault.

Another set of effusive thanks goes to my editor, Amy Sun, who, like her name suggests, was a bright warm spot of support, insightful comments, and brilliant fixes.

My girlfriends Joanne Russell, Tracy Rapp, Anna Crean, Sheila Berger, Nicolaia Rips, Martina Forman, and Lorna Graham, who fed me dinner, listened to my endless whining, and read my essays, deserve a shout-out.

A heartfelt thanks to my stepsons and their families, who could have been "baggage" from a former life, but instead turned out to be my most precious gifts.

The biggest thanks, of course, goes to my boys, Jonathan and Oliver. They became my whole world when the world shut down, and held me and comforted me as I had done for them when they were little. They stepped into the task of growing up overnight when Ric died. They read my essays, and allowed me my truth. What amazing men we raised. Half that credit is my husband's.

Lastly, my thanks to Maria Shriver, a woman I have long admired. I'm truly honored to have been asked to participate in her desire to shine kindness and light into the world with her imprint.